6ᵀᴴ FORM   6 TH. FORM

GW00806292

A CONCISE DICTIONARY OF
ENGLISH
slang

TEACH YOURSELF

A CONCISE DICTIONARY OF
ENGLISH
slang

B. A. Phythian

Hodder & Stoughton
LONDON SYDNEY AUCKLAND

British Library Cataloguing in Publication Data

Concise Dictionary of English Slang. –
New ed of 3 Rev. ed
  I. Phythian, B. A.
  427.09
ISBN 0 340 58743 1

First published 1955
Third edition 1986
First *Teach Yourself* edition 1993

Typeset by Rowland Phototypesetting Ltd,
Bury St Edmunds, Suffolk
Printed in Great Britain for the educational publishing
division of Hodder & Stoughton Ltd, Mill Road, Dunton Green,
Sevenoaks, Kent by Clays Ltd, St Ives plc.

Preface

Slang is a very elusive element in human communication. It enters the language from a wide variety of sources, often from closely knit communities such as the armed forces or cockney culture. There are many countries where English is native, all of which add their own contributions to the store of slang, as they also enrich Standard English, helping to make it one of the most complex and developing of the world's languages. Sometimes the new slang, like the old, drops out of use, quickly or gradually. Where it remains, it may remain as slang, temporarily or for a long period, or it may develop into something else, at varying speeds. The normal development is for a slang expression to become accepted into that large body of more 'educated' but still informal English known as colloquialism, and thence into the full status of Standard English—which can be most briefly defined as those words and expressions not classified as 'slang' or 'colloquialism' in the standard dictionaries.

It may be seen, then, that at any one time it can be extremely difficult to determine the exact status of a word or expression, because language is alive and changing and slang is one of its most volatile components. This is especially true in our own century, when the cinema, newspapers and television have made language more accessible and carried it from continent to continent more quickly than ever before. An additional problem is that words often used by dictionary-makers when defining categories of language – such as 'formal', 'educated', 'accepted' – are themselves even less clear-cut now than they used to be. English in the twentieth century has become more and more informal, reflecting the ever-increasing informality in our society.

Both slang and colloquialism belong to this category of informal English, the sort used daily in conversation and writing whenever the occasion does not demand more studied vocabulary, structures or tone of voice. The difference between informal and formal English is the difference in language between the letter to a friend and a business letter, the TV game-show and the serious documentary film, the gossip column and the leader column, the pub and the pulpit. Such differences are not as distinct as they used to be: business correspondence is no longer conducted in stiff and pompous terms, and parsons, like politicians and leader-writers, feel it necessary to reach for more populist language than they once used. Even so, we still tend to need a different language and style for different occasions and purposes: what we want to say, our relationship with those we say it to, and the circumstances in which we say it are among the factors that determine whether we use formal or informal English.

So the difference between the two is not a matter of 'good' and 'bad' English. Bad English is that which is slovenly, not clear, ungrammatical, unnecessarily wordy, and unsuited to its purpose. Slang and colloquialism are perfectly 'good' English as long as they are used in appropriate contexts. Slang, being the more informal of the two, is normally reserved for occasions when one is sure of one's audience or readership. It is spicy, often humorous, sometimes vulgar, and occasionally novel and therefore obscure. It is used only when these qualities will not impair communication, give offence, or imply an unintended lack of seriousness. Colloquial English is less informal: it is correct and acceptable in dealings with people one knows or can expect to be on level terms with, but it is still sufficiently racy or casual to make it unsuitable for occasions when a neutral or conventional tone is needed.

In compiling this volume I have been guided by two criteria: firstly, slang has been emphasised at the expense of colloquialism, because the former is less frequently recorded in generally available form; secondly, I have tried to confine myself largely to current usage.

As for the alphabetic arrangement, if an entry consists of an expression of several words, it has been placed where I think the reader would most expect to find it, i.e. under the key word, with cross-references in cases where several words in the expression seem to be of equal importance. Complete cross-referring would have been impossible, however, without increasing the size of the book very considerably, and I hope the reader will be prepared to look for such an expression in more than one place if it does not appear in what seems the obvious one.

Keston, June 1985

B. A. Phythian

Abbreviations

Abbr.	Abbreviation
adj.	Adjective
adv.	Adverb
App.	Applied to
Derog.	Derogatory
Dil.	Dilution
Emph.	Emphatic; emphasis
Esp.	Especially
Ex.	Originating in
Excl.	Exclamation
Facet.	Facetious
Gen.	General; generally
Juv.	Juvenile
Lit.	Literally
Met.	Metaphorically
n.	Noun
Neg.	Negative
Occ.	Occasionally
Old f.	Old fashioned
Opp.	Opposite
Or.	Originally; origin
Pop.	Popular (see **pop** in dictionary)
RS	Rhyming Slang
Theat.	Theatrical
usu.	Usually
v.	Verb
WWI & II	World War I & II

* For the guidance of users of this dictionary whose native language is not English, an asterisk has been placed after certain entries which are generally regarded as obscenities.

Acknowledgements

Any work on slang naturally owes much to the standard authority on the subject, Eric Partridge's monumental and very accurate *Dictionary of Slang and Unconventional English* (7th edition, 1970). I gladly record my own indebtedness to these incomparable volumes, and my thanks for the pleasure they have afforded.

My own work began as a revision of William Freeman's *Concise Dictionary of Slang*, but so little of this now remains in these pages that it would be wrong to hold him responsible for them. It would be equally wrong, however, not to acknowledge his responsibility for the original conception and for some of the entries.

I am grateful to Joyce Hytner, Simon Powell, Harold Frayman and Peggie Patrick for colourful suggestions, and to Stella Lister for patient and expert typing of the manuscript.

B.A.P.

Acknowledgements

A

A First class.

A over T* See **arse over tip**. [Abbr.]

AWOL Absent without official leave. (Military)

abdabs, give one the
1. Make one irritable or annoyed.
2. See also **screaming abdabs**.
3. Occ. **habdabs**.

about one, have something Have some quality which makes one attractive.

about right Approximately correct.

about the size of Approximately correct.

about time At last. Not before the appropriate time.

above board Honest. Frank. Unconcealed.

above par In good health and spirits.

absolutely Emph. expression of agreement.

accidentally on purpose Deliberately, with an attempt to pretend otherwise.

account for Kill.

ace
1. Person of outstanding ability (usu. in sport).
2. [adj.] Very expert.
3. [adj.] Excellent.

acid
1. The drug LSD.
2. **come the acid** Exaggerate. Speak sarcastically.

acid-head One who takes LSD.

ackers Money.

across, get Irritate. Annoy.

act, get into the Thrust oneself into.

act together, get one's Behave consistently. Succeed by one's efforts. Agree.

act your age Behave in a manner appropriate to your age, not to that of a much younger person.

action, a piece of the Participation. Share of success or activity.

ad Advertisement. Also **advert**.

ad(-)lib
1. Speak without script. Improvise (e.g. when playing music).
2. As many or much as one chooses.

Adam, not know (someone) from Not know (person) at all.

Adam's ale Water.

add up Make sense.
   • *It doesn't add up.*

adrift Uninformed.

aerated Angrily excited.

afeard Afraid.

affair Gen. term for almost any object or happening.

after a fashion In a way (usu. not the best one).

after the Lord Mayor's show (comes the dust-, muck- *or* **shit-cart)** Derisive reference to any anti-climax.

after you with When you have finished may I have . . . ?

afters Sweet course at a meal.

ages, for For a long time. Also **for an age**.

aggro Stirring up of trouble (usu. violent). Inflammatory behaviour. Fighting. (Abbr. aggravation.)

agin Against.

agony See **pile on the agony**.

agony column Part of newspaper, magazine, etc., devoted to readers' personal problems.

aid of, in
1. For.
2. **what's (all) that in aid of?** What does that mean? What is it for?

air, hot Empty talk.

air, in the Likely to happen. Under discussion. Rumoured.

air was blue, the There was a good deal of bad language.

airy-fairy Light, insubstantial, lacking in common sense; not closely connected with reality (usu. of ideas, plans, etc.).
akkas See **ackers**.

alarm and despondency Depression. Anxiety. [Emph.]

alibi [n.] Excuse.

alive and kicking Sprightly. In good health.

alive, look Make haste.

all Very.
  - *I am all confused.*

all along the line Everywhere. At every stage. Incessantly.

all at sea Bewildered.

all chiefs and no Indians All leaders and no subordinates.

all dressed up and nowhere to go Expression signifying frustration connected with failure of social event.

all ends up In every respect. Easily.

all for (it) Entirely in favour of (it).

all hands
1. Everyone in the particular group referred to.
2. **all hands to the pumps** Everyone working to cope with emergency.

all hell broke (*or* was let) loose There was great uproar, fuss, dissension, etc.

all hot and bothered Very agitated, excited, nervous, confused.

all in Completely exhausted.

all my eye (and Betty Martin) Nonsense.

all of as much as.
- *He was all of two hours late.*

all of a dither In a state of excitement, anxiety, confusion, bewilderment, etc.

all of a tiswas (tizwas) Very agitated and/or confused.

all of a tremble Trembling with fear, excitement, etc.

all out
1. Making every effort.
2. **go all out** Make every effort.

all over
1. Completely covered with.
2. Ended. Usu. **it's all over with** It has ended.
3. Emph. for characteristic behaviour.
   - *That's Simon all over.*
4. **all over the place** *or* **shop** *or* **auction** In a state of confusion or untidiness.

all present and correct All correct.

all right
1. Gen. expression of assent or acceptance.
2. **a bit of all right** Person or thing approved of.

all right on the night, will be Will be correct in time for the appropriate occasion.

all set Ready and willing.

all that
1. Very.
   - *He's clever, but not all that clever.*
2. All that sort of thing.

all that jazz All that sort of thing.

all the best I wish you the best of luck.

all the fun of the fair Plenty of amusement.

all the go The fashion. Popular.

all the rage Fashionable.

all the world and his wife Everybody.

all there
1. Alert. Shrewd. Efficient.
2. **not all there** Mentally deficient.

all thumbs Clumsy with one's hands.

all time
1. Of all time.
2. **all-time high** *or* **low** A record level of height or depth.
   - *Prices have reached an all-time high.* Prices have never been higher.

all to cock Very confused, mixed-up, unsatisfactory.

all to pieces *or* **pot** In a confused or unsatisfactory state. In a condition of mental or physical collapse.

all to the good Entirely beneficial.

all up *or* **U.P.** Finished. Ruined.

all very fine and large *or* **dandy** Ironic term of approval.

all very well Qualified expression of agreement (usu. followed by but or if).

almighty Very considerable.

altogether, in the In the nude.

amidships In the solar plexus.

ammo. Ammunition. [Abbr.]

anchors Brakes.

and all that And all such things.

and how! I do agree!

and no mistake! Emph. addition to sentence.

and the rest Sarcastic rejoinder, suggesting that the previous speaker has been less than frank.

and you Contemptuous rejoinder to insult.

angel Financial supporter of a business, often theat.

angle Distort (usu. a story or argument).

animal, there's no such There is no such person or thing.

anno domini Increasing effects of old age.

answer is a lemon, the No. (Dismissive or abusive or facet. negative reply.)

answer to a maiden's prayer Attractive man.

ants in one's pants, have Be restless or excited.

any amount A great deal.

any how Carelessly; without thought.
* *The books were scattered about any how or anyhow.*

any more for any more? Does anyone want more?

any, not have Not agree.

any old . . .
1. Any . . . whatever.
2. **any old how** By any method. (Emph. for any how.)
3. **any old thing** *or* **way** Anything, any way. [Emph.]

any port in a storm Any refuge will suit in an emergency.

any road Any way.

anything goes Nothing is forbidden.

anything, like Very. Much.

apple-pie order Perfect order or condition.

apron-strings, tied to Dominated by woman.

are you fit? Are you ready?

are you with me? Do you understand me? Do you agree with me?

'arf a mo Half a moment.

argue the toss Argue, often fiercely.

argy-bargy Dispute.

ark, come out of the Be extremely old.

arm, as long as one's Very long.

arrows Darts.

arse*
1. Buttocks. Posterior.
2. Also used loosely to signify any rear part. Also **arse-end**.
3. **arse about** [v.] Waste time. Behave ineffectually.
4. **arse-crawler** *or* **-licker** Sycophant.
5. **arse over tip** *or* **tit** Head over heels.
6. **arse up** [v.] Perform unsuccessfully. Bungle.
7. **arse-hole** Anus. **arse-holes** Vulgar excl. of contempt.
8. **from arse-hole to breakfast time** All the time.
9. **my arse** Used in numerous expressions signifying incredulity.

arsy varsy *or* **versy** Topsy turvy. Back to front. Upside down.

artic Articulated lorry (i.e. one with detachable driving cab).

arty Having the affectations supposedly proper to artists. (Abbr. Artistic.)

arty-crafty Artistic but not practical.

as . . . as they come *or* **make them** Expression of emph.
• *He's as daft as they come.* He is extremely foolish.

as different as chalk from cheese Utterly different.

as ever is Emph. addition to statement.

as long as one's arm Very long.

as plain as the nose on one's face Very obvious.

as sure as eggs is eggs Very certain.

as the actress said to the bishop (or vice versa) Added to an innocent remark to add sexual innuendo to it.

as they come *or* **make them** As it is possible to be.

as you were Expression of mild apology for a mistake the speaker has just made in something he has said.

ashes, win the Win a series of England v. Australia test matches at cricket, etc. Also **lose, regain the ashes**, etc.

ask for (it) Take action (usu. foolish) leading almost inevitably and knowingly to an undesired result.

ask me another! I don't know.

ass* Evasion of **arse**.

at a loose end Temporarily unoccupied.

at a pinch In an emergency.

at long last After a lengthy lapse of time.

at sea Confused. Unenlightened.

at that Moreover.
- *The meal was expensive, and cold at that.*

attaboy! Excl. of encouragement or approval.

Aunt Fanny Used in numerous expressions as emph. excl. to indicate derision, disbelief or negation.

Aunt Sally Person or thing attacked merely for the sake of attacking (usu. consciously made into such a target).

Aunty *or* **Auntie** The British Broadcasting Corporation.

away with, get Succeed. Do something with impunity.

awfully Very.

awkward squad
1. Untrained recruits.
2. Uncooperative people.

axe
1. [v.] Dismiss (e.g. from employment, usu. because superfluous).
2. [v.] Severely reduce (usu. of costs, prices, etc.).
3. Remove.

B

B [Abbr.] Bastard *or* bugger.

BF [Abbr.] Bloody fool.

baby
1. Term of address, usu. affectionate (but becoming so over used that it is nearly colourless). [Pop.]
2. **one's baby** One's responsibility, concern, interest.
   - *It's not my baby.*
3. Sweetheart.

baby-snatcher Person who marries someone very much younger.

baby with the bathwater, throw out the Be over-zealous, esp. in reform or change, so that the valuable is disposed of as well as the less valuable.

baccy Tobacco.

back-answer Impudent reply.

back, be *or* **get on one's**
1. Supervise one closely. Apply pressure. Bully one.
2. [Opp.] **get off one's back**.

back-chat Impudent reply or replies.

back-handed compliment Same as **left-handed compliment**.

back-hander
1. Tip or bribe.
2. (Unexpected) blow with back of the hand.

back-lash [n.] Violent reaction.

back number Person with out-of-date ideas or attitudes.

back of beyond, the Somewhere remote and difficult of access.

back of, break the Complete the biggest or most difficult part of (a task, etc.).

back of one's neck, talk through the Talk nonsense.

back-pedal Withdraw from previously adopted position. Stop. Pause.

back-room boys Workers whose efforts, though vital, receive no publicity or general recognition.

back-scratch
1. Flatter.
2. **back-scratcher** Sycophant.
3. **back-scratching** Sycophancy.

back-seat driver Person who gives unwanted advice to someone in charge.

back seat, take a Adopt a position which is not prominent.

back teeth See **fed**.

back to square one Back to where one started.

back up [v.] Support. Encourage. Be ready to help.

back-up
1. [n.] Support.
2. [adj.] Supporting.

back up, get *or* **put one's** Annoy one.

backside Posterior.

backward in coming forward Shy.

bacon, bring home the Succeed in doing something.

bad books, in one's In disgrace.

bad egg Untrustworthy person.

bad about something, feel Be regretful.

bad form Manners, habits, conventions, not conforming to those of polite society.

bad hat Rascal.

bad job, a Unfortunate.

bad lot Untrustworthy person.

bad-mouth [v.] Criticise personally.

bad news Disagreeable person.

bad, not Quite good.

bad, not half Fairly good.

bad old days The relatively disagreeable past. (Often used ironically.)

bad shot Wrong guess.

bad show, a Unfortunate.

bad, to the In deficit.

bad, too Unfortunate (but unavoidable and thus needing to be tolerated).

bad trip, be on *or* **have a** Experience very unpleasant effects from drug-taking. [Pop.]

baddie (or-**y**) Villain (usu. in film, etc.).

bag
1. [v.] Take. Seize. (Usu. before someone else does.)
2. [n.] Unattractive woman (usu. past her prime). Often **old bag** Disagreeable old woman.

bag, in the All arranged. Very likely to happen. Virtually certain.

bag of bones, a Very thin.

bag of tricks, the (whole) Everything.

bag, pull something out of the Discover a means of achieving success, usu. belatedly.

bags
1. Trousers.
2. **bags I** I claim. [Juv.]

bags of A lot of.

baggage Pert woman.

bait [n.] Rage.

baked, half- Incomplete. Muddled. Not fully thought out.

baker's dozen Thirteen.

baking Very hot. (Of weather.)

bald as a billiard ball *or* **coot** Entirely bald.

bald-headed, go (at it) Act rashly and whole-heartedly.

ball-game State of affairs. Usu. **a whole new ball-game** An entirely new state of affairs.

ball, have a Have an enjoyable time.

ball of fire Energetic and spirited person.

ball, on the Efficient. Alert.

ball, play Co-operate.

ball rolling See **keep (start) the ball rolling**.

ball up [v.] Bungle.

ballock(s) See **bollock**.

balloon goes up, the
1. The proceedings begin.
2. Trouble begins.

balls*
1. Testicles.
2. Vulgar excl. of contempt.
3. Nonsense.
4. Spirit. Courage.
5. See **brass monkey** *and* **make a balls(-up) of.**

balls chewed (off), get one's* Receive a severe reprimand.

balls to . . .* A dismissive expression.

balls (something) up* [v.] Do wrongly, creating muddle.

balls-up* Confusion. Muddle.

bally Polite evasion of **bloody**.

ballyhoo Noisy and vulgar publicity.

baloney See **boloney**.

bamboozle [v.] Swindle. Deceive. Mystify.

bananas, go Become mad, wild, angry.

bandwagon
1. Popular movement or fashion.
2. **jump on** *or* **join the bandwagon** Favour something or someone when public esteem has already been granted. Join a fashion (usu. for fashion's sake).

bang
1. [n.] Drug injection.
2. *[v.] Have sexual intercourse. Also [n.]
3. **full bang** Full speed.
4. **bang goes** . . . There goes . . .
   • *Bang goes another week's wages.*
5. **with a bang** Very successfully.
6. [adv.] Completely. Exactly.
   • *Sitting bang in the middle of the row.*

bang on
1. Very accurate.
2. [v.] Talk volubly.

bang, the whole The whole. [Emph.] Usu. **the whole bang shoot** The whole lot.

banger
1. Sausage.
2. Old (noisy) motor-car.

banjax Ruin. Inconvenience.

bar the shouting Virtually. Usu. **all over bar the shouting** Virtually finished.

barbs Barbiturate drug.

barge
1. [v.] Behave, usu. move, roughly or clumsily.
2. **barge in** Interfere, intrude (rudely).
3. **barge into** Collide (clumsily).
4. **barge about** Move around roughly.

barge-pole, wouldn't touch it with a Will have nothing to do with it.

bark
1. [n.] Cough.
2. **bark up the wrong tree** Act under a misapprehension.

barmy Crazy. Eccentric.

barn-door Something very wide.

barn-storming
1. [n.] Ranting behaviour.
2. [adj.] Ranting.

barney [n.] Quarrel.

barrack-room lawyer Person not in authority who claims to know all the rules, or creates difficulties by quoting them.

barrel, have one over a Put in a serious predicament, so that one is unable to retaliate.

barrow boy Street trader selling goods from barrow.

bash
1. Strike (heavily). Also **bash up** Assault.
2. **bash into** Crash into.
3. **have a bash** Make an attempt.
4. **give something a bash** Strike something a blow. Attempt something.
5. **bash on** Go on (usu. doggedly).
6. [n.] Celebration. Party.

bashing Heavy defeat or criticism, e.g. **union-bashing** Severe and persistent criticism of Trades Unions.

bashing, take a Suffer heavy defeat or criticism.

basinful, a
1. An excess (of work, trouble, excitement, etc.).
2. **have** *or* **get a basinful of** Look avidly at. Make an attempt at.

basket Polite evasion of **bastard**.

bastard*
1. Any unpleasant or irritating object, situation, etc.
2. Term of abuse, with no implication of real meaning. Disagreeable person. (Can also be used without abuse, to mean 'fellow' e.g.
   - *You lucky bastard.*)

bat along Move easily or quickly (usu. of car).

bat, off one's own Independently.

bat on a sticky wicket Be in difficulties.

bat out of hell, like a Very quickly.

bats, be Be crazy or eccentric. Also **have bats in the belfry.**

bate Same as **bait.**

batter, on the On a spree (usu. drunken).

battle-axe Formidable woman.

batty Mad. Eccentric.

bawl out Reprimand harshly, often publicly.

bay window Prominent stomach.

be a devil! Take a risk. [Facet.]

be my guest! Yes, certainly. (Facet. response to a request.)

be off (with you)! Go away.

beak Magistrate. Schoolmaster.

beam, broad in the Wide-hipped.

beam, off (the) Wrong. On the wrong track. [adj.] **off-beam.**

beam-ends, on one's Worn out. In difficulty. Short of money.

bean
1. Small sum of money.
2. **not to have a bean** Be without money.
3. **not worth a bean** Worth very little.

bean-feast Good time (usu. with eating).

bean, old Affectionate, slightly old-fashioned form of address.

beano Jollification.

beans, give someone Rebuke or punish someone. *See also* **full of beans** and **spill the beans.**

bear Gruff person.

bear-garden Scene of confusion and noise.

bear with a sore head, like a Ill-tempered.

beastly Unpleasant. Detestable. (But in certain contexts, usu. juv., can be quite mild.)

beat [Abbr.] **beatnik.**

beat about the bush Approach the subject in an indirect way. Hesitate. Prevaricate.

beat cock-fighting
1. Be surprising.
2. Be exciting or extremely enjoyable.

beat it
1. Go away.
2. **can you beat it** *or* **that?** What could be more surprising?

beat, off- Unconventional.

beat one's head against a brick wall Fail to progress. Reach dead-lock. Encounter insurmountable or frustrating difficulties.

beat the band Surpass everything.

beat the living daylights out of Thrash severely.

beat to a frazzle Be very superior to.

beatnik General term loosely covering young people with unorthodox ways of life, dress, hair-style, habits, tastes, etc. Also **drop-out, hippy.**

beaut [Abbr.] Beauty.

beauty sleep [n.] Sleep before midnight.

beaver, eager Zealous (or slightly over-zealous) person.

bed on the wrong side, get out of Be irritable.

beddy-byes Sleep. [Juv.]

Bedfordshire Bed. [Juv.] Often **up the wooden hill to Bedfordshire** Upstairs to bed. [Juv.]

bedpost See **you, me and the bedpost**.

bed-sit(ter) Single living-room with bed.

bedworthy Sexually attractive.

bee's knees, the Something or someone excellent in every way.

Beeb British Broadcasting Corporation.

beef
1. [n.] Complaint.
2. [v.] Complain.
3. **put beef into** Work hard at.
4. **beef up** Strengthen.

beefcake Display of attractive male body.

been and gone and done it Done it. [Facet.]

beer and skittles, all Entirely pleasant.

beer, on the Over-addicted to drinking beer. On a drinking spree.

beer, small [n.] Insignificant matter. [adj.] Trifling.

beer-up Drinking spree.

beetle off Depart.

beezer Person. Nose.

before you can say Jack Robinson *or* **knife** Instantly.

beggar
1. Polite evasion of **bugger**.
2. Fellow.

beggar for . . . , a One who very much enjoys . . .

begin to, not to Emph. negative.
- *His statement doesn't begin to answer the question.* He has not answered the question at all.

bell Phone call. usu. **give one a bell**.

bell, sound as a In excellent health or condition.

belly-ache
1. [v.] Grumble.
2. [n.] Pain in the stomach.

belly-button Navel.

belly-flop Dive (or fall) in which one lands on one's belly.

bellyful Enough. Too much.
- *I've had a bellyful of him.* I have reached the end of my patience with him.

belly-laugh Loud spontaneous laugh.

below the belt
1. Unfair(ly), often because unexpected(ly).
2. **hit below the belt** Act unfairly.

belt
1. [n.] Blow.
2. [v.] Strike.
3. **belt (along)** Move quickly.
4. **belt it** Go away.
5. **belt up** Be quiet. Stop talking. Fasten safety belt.
6. **under one's belt** To one's credit.
   - *Six years' experience under my belt.*
7. **belt out** Utter forcibly.
8. **full belt** Full speed.

belter Excellent thing or person.

belting
1. [n.] Beating.
2. [adj.] Very good.

bend
1. Damage (usu. a car).
2. **bend over backwards** Go to considerable trouble, show considerable flexibility (usu. to accommodate some person or thing).
3. See **round the bend**.
4. [v.] Pervert.

bender
1. Heavy bout of drinking.
2. Sexual pervert.
3. **on one's benders** Exhausted.

bending, catch someone Take someone at a disadvantage.

bends, the Sickness caused by rapid recompression of air.

bennies Benzedrine tablets.

bent
1. Damaged. (From **bend**.)
2. Perverted.
3. Criminal.

berk Foolish or unpleasant person.

best [v.] Gain an advantage over.

best bib and tucker Best clothes.

best foot forward *or* **foremost, put one's** Walk quickly. Make utmost endeavour.

best of a bad job, make the Do as well as one can in unfavourable circumstances.

best of British (luck), the Good luck to you. (usu. ironical.)

best, of the
1. Of a certain thing.
2. Of the best kind. See **best, one of the**.

best, one of the A kind or agreeable fellow.

bet
1. Be certain.
   - *I bet he's forgotten.*
2. **You bet.** You may be certain.
3. [n.] Opinion.
   - *My bet is that . . .*

bet, best Best thing to do.

bet one's boots *or* **bottom dollar** *or* **life**
1. Be entirely certain.
2. See **you bet**.

better half Wife.

better hole (or go to) More congenial place.

better than a slap (poke) in the eye *or* **in the belly with a wet fish** *or* **lettuce** Fairly acceptable. Better than nothing. Also **better than a kick in the pants** *or* **up the arse***.

between the devil and the deep (blue) sea Caught between two equally disagreeable alternatives. Also **between two fires**.

between you and me and the bed- *or* **gate-post** In confidence.

betwixt and between Indecisive. Midway.

bevvy [n.] Drink. Also **bevvied** *or* **bevied (up)** Drunk.

bezazz Strong personal impact esp. of performer.

bible, the The book or document containing any rules, regulations, instructions, etc.

bible-puncher *or* **-thumper** Aggressively religious person (usu. proselytizer).

biddy Elderly woman.

biff
1. [v.] Strike heavily.
2. [n.] Heavy blow.

big
1. Important. Outstanding.
2. **look** *or* **talk big** Try to appear important.
3. adj. of ironical approval. See **big deal**.
4. [adv.] On a big scale. **think big** Have bold plans.
5. **too big for one's boots** Conceited.
6. Ambitious.
   * *to have big plans.*
7. **Big Bertha** Enormous German cannon in WWI.
8. **go over big** Succeed. Enjoy popularity.

big boy Mock-deferential term of address.

big bug, chief *or* **daddy** Bigwig.

big cheese Important person in his own particular sphere.

big deal! Sarcastic excl. of approval or surprise.

big gun Same as **big cheese**.

big hand See **give a big hand**.

big head, have a Be conceited.

big-head [n.] Conceited person. [adj.] **big-headed** Conceited.

big idea, what's the What is going on?

big-mouth One who talks too loudly or too much.

big noise *or* **shot** Important person.

big soft Nellie Simpleton.

big stuff
1. Anything important.
2. Excl. to greet or comment on something important. (occ. ironically.)

big talk Arrogant talk.

big time (in the)
1. Enjoying success. (Usu. of entertainers.)
2. **hit the big time** Achieve success.
3. **big-time** [adj.] Successful.

big way, in a Very considerably. In an elaborate or ambitious style. With enthusiasm. Often **go over in a big way** Enjoy considerable success.

bike [n.] & [v.] Bicycle. Motor cycle.

bilge Nonsense.

Bill, the The Police. A policeman.

bill and coo Talk amorously or in very friendly manner.

billet Job. Position. Situation.

billy-(h)o or o(h), like Emph. addition to sentence.
   ● *Rain like billy-o.* Rain very heavily.

bind, a
   1. [n.] Extremely dull, tiresome, boring person or thing.
   2. [v.] Bore. Irritate. **bind rigid** Bore heartily.
   3. [v.] Grumble (habitually).

binge
   1. Period of heavy drinking.
   2. **on a binge** Indulging in drinking bout.

bingo! Excl. indicating success or completion.

bint Girl (not usu. polite).

bird
   1. Young woman. Girl-friend.
   2. Person. Thus **a funny, queer bird**, etc. A strange person.
   3. **do bird** Serve a prison sentence. **bird-lime** Time spent in prison.
   4. **get (give) the bird** Receive (express) the dissatisfaction of an unappreciative audience. Be dismissed.
   5. **a little bird told me** I heard from a secret source.

bird-cage, mouth like the bottom of a Dry, unpleasant-tasting mouth (e.g. on day after excessive drinking).

birds, strictly for the Uninteresting.

birthday suit, in one's Naked.

biscuit, take the Surpass everything (usu. in causing surprise).

bish Mistake.

bit
1. Small coin.
2. **a (little) bit** A short while. Somewhat.
3. **have a bit*** Copulate.
4. See **side**.
5. **bit-part actor** Actor with insignificant role.
6. **bit steep, stiff** *or* **thick** Rather excessive.
7. Aspect of things (Very loose usage).
   - *I quite like the holiday arrangements but I don't like the sailing bit.*

bit much, a An unacceptable or offensive incident, state of affairs, etc.

bit of all right, a Highly satisfying.

bit of doing, take a Be difficult to accomplish.

bit of fluff, skirt, stuff, etc. Sexually attractive woman.

bit off, a
1. A slight reduction.
2. Slightly sour.
3. Same as **bit much, a**.

bitch
1. [n.] Extremely unpleasant woman. [adj.] **bitchy** Spiteful.
2. [v.] Complain querulously.
3. **bitch up** Muddle.

bite
1. [n.] Pungency. Sting. Impact. Excitement.
2. [v.] **what's biting** *or* **bitten (you,** etc.)? What's the matter with (you, etc.)?

bite the dust Come to an end (usu. suddenly and unpleasantly).

bits and pieces Possessions.
   Also **bits and bobs**.

bitten Obsessed.

bivvy [n.] Temporary camp. [v.] Make temporary camp, usu. in small tent in remote area.

biz
1. Business.
2. **show biz** The entertainment industry.

blabber-mouth One who talks too much or unguardedly.

black
1. Mistake. Usu. **put up a black** Make an error.
2. Negro. Also **the blacks** (not polite).
3. **in the black** In credit (of bank account, etc.).
4. **in black and white** In writing.
5. **black mark** Sign of disapproval. (Slightly facet.)
   - *You'll get a black mark if you do that.* You ought not to do that.

black as the ace of spades Very black. Very dirty.

black jack Cosh.

black leg
1. [n.] Worker who refuses to go out on strike. Also [adj.].
2. [v.] Boycott.

black man, the The devil.

black market Illegal source of supply for rare goods.

black out [v.] Faint.

black-out [n.]
1. Unconsciousness following faint.
2. Censorship.
   - *A news black-out.* No news (e.g. because of government decree).

black sheep (of the family) Person in disgrace or distrusted (in eyes of his own family).

black-shirt Fascist.

black velvet Mixture of champagne and stout.

blah
1. [n.] Wordy nonsense.
2. [v.] Speak wordy nonsense.

blanket(t)y blank Polite evasion of stronger words, esp. **bloody hell**.

blarney Cajolery. Flattery.

blast! Excl. of annoyance, often with other words, e.g. **blast it! blast and damnation!**, etc.

blast, at full At full speed. Working hard.

blasted Emph. adj. expressing disapproval, annoyance. Evasion of **bloody**.

blazes, go to
1. Emph. refusal.
2. Go away. Go to hell.
3. **to blazes with** . . . I have no interest in . . .

blazes, the (blue) Emph. addition to **what? who? how?**
- *What the blazes are you doing?*

bleat [n.] & [v.] Grumble.

bleed Ruin by extortion or victimisation (usu. financial). Emph. **bleed white**.

bleed like a (stuck) pig Bleed copiously.

bleeder Person (usu. derog.).

bleeding Meaningless adj. or adv. to add emph. Also adv. **bleeding well** Evasion of **bloody**.

bless him (etc.)! Expression of affection. Also **bless his** (etc.) **heart** *or* **(little) cotton socks**.

bless my soul! Excl. of surprise.

bless one's stars Be profoundly grateful.

bless you!
1. Emph. form of thanks.
2. Traditional response to someone who sneezes.

blessed *or* **blest, (well) I'm**
1. Excl. of surprise.
2. Emph. neg. asseveration.
- *I'm blessed if I'll do it.* I will certainly not do it.

blew in See blow (4).

blighter
1. Person.
2. Person mildly disapproved of.

Blighty England.

Blimp, (Colonel) Strict, conservative, narrow-minded or conventional (usu. retired) officer. Pompous establishment figure. [adj.] **blimpish**.

blim(e)y, (cor *or* **gor)** Mild expletive.

blind
1. [v.] Curse. See **eff and blind**.
2. Intoxicated. Usu. **blind drunk** Very drunk.
3. [v.] Go ahead thoughtlessly and carelessly.
4. [n.] Drinking spree. Usu. **go on a blind**.
5. **swear blind** Swear solemnly.
6. **go (into something) blind** Enter (an undertaking) on inadequate information.

blind bit of notice, not to take a To pay no attention.

blind date Assignation with unknown person of opp. sex.

blind one with science Overwhelm, confuse (or simply present) one with superior knowledge. Thus **blinded with** *or* **by science**.

blind side
1. Weakest point.
2. **on the blind side** At the weakest point. Unexpectedly.

blinder
1. Person or thing very much approved of.
2. **play a blinder** Perform exceptionally well (usu. in a game).

blink, on the (Of machines) Not functioning properly.

blinking Mild adj. of emph. (Mainly juv.)

blister Annoying person.

blithering
1. Foolish.
2. Mild adj. expressing annoyance. Usu. **blithering idiot**.

blitz
1. [n.] Heavy bombing raid. Also [v.].
2. [n.] Intensive action, usu. to remedy a fault.
   • *The police are having a blitz on illegal parking in the village.*

blob Score of nought (usu. in cricket).

block Head. Usu. **knock one's block off** Strike one.

block, off one's Mad.

blockbuster Anything large, threatening or comprehensively demoralising.
   • *The exam paper had a few blockbusters in it.*

bloke Fellow.

blondie Person with blonde hair.

blood-bath Event causing many casualties.

blood chit Written permission.

blood and thunder Sensational book, film, etc.

blood-wagon Ambulance.

bloody Adj. or adv. of emphasis.

bloody hell Common oath. Also much used for emph.
- *What the bloody hell does he think he's doing?* Whatever is he doing?

bloody-minded Obstinate. Deliberately uncooperative, obstructive or unreasonable.

bloomer Mistake.

bloomers Knickers.

blooming Mild adj. or adv. of emphasis.

blooper Embarrassing mistake.

blot one's copy-book Mar one's good reputation.

blotto Drunk.

blow
1. Mild excl. of surprise or annoyance. Also **blow me!, blow me down!, blow it!, oh blow!**, etc.
2. **I'll be** (*or* **I'm**) **blowed if I'll** . . . I will not . . .
3. Go away. Depart suddenly.
4. **blow in** Visit casually and unexpectedly.
5. **look what the wind's blown in!** See who's arrived! (Facet. greeting.)
6. Spend money recklessly.
7. [n.] Fellatio*. Also **blow-job**.
8. [v.] Fail in an attempt. Also **blow one's chances, blow it**.

blow great guns (Of wind) Blow powerfully.

blow off steam Dissipate surplus energy or anger, etc., by violent speech or activity.

blow one's mind Achieve or experience ecstasy or oblivion (usu. by music, drugs, etc.). [Pop.]

blow one's stack *or* **top** Lose one's temper.

blow-out [n.] Large meal.

blow sky-high Refute utterly.

blow the gaff Reveal a secret.

blow up [v.]
1. Lose one's temper.
2. Reprimand severely.

blow-up [n.]
1. Quarrel.
2. Photographic enlargement.

blow you, Jack Expression of unconcern.

blower Telephone.

blub Weep.

blue
1. Indecent. Obscene.
2. See **air was blue**.
3. Miserable. Depressed. **the blues** Feelings of depression.

blue-arsed fly, like a* Emph. addition to several verbs expressing movement (e.g. **run around**) to suggest agitation.

blue-eyed boy Favourite.

blue funk, in a Very frightened.

blue in Spend (rashly).

blue murder
1. Sounds indicating anger or terror.
2. **cry blue murder** Make a great fuss.
3. **there'll be blue murder if** . . . There will be considerable uproar or trouble if . . .

blue, out of the Suddenly, without warning.

blue pencil
1. Pencil used to censor a piece of writing.
2. **blue-pencil** [v.] Censor.

blurb Any short piece of explanatory writing. (Often advertisement, e.g. on wrapper of book.)

board, take on Consider. Reckon with.

boards, the The stage.

boat See **rock the boat**.

boat, miss the Be too late. Lose an opportunity.

boat out, push the Spend money (usu. generously).

bob Shilling (now 5p).

Bob's your uncle All is satisfactorily completed.

bobble [v.] Move with frequent but slight up-and-down motion.

bobby Policeman.

bobby dazzler Sparkling, dazzling person or thing.

bobby-soxer Adolescent girl following teenage fashions [Old f.].

Boche German. [Derog.]

bod Person.

boffin Research scientist.

bog, bogs
 1. Lavatory. Also **bog-house**.
 2. **have a bog** Use the lavatory.
 3. **bog** [v.] Defecate.

bog-eyed Looking very tired.

bog-house barrister Same as **barrack-room lawyer**.

bog-Irish Irish. [Derog.]

bog(e)y Policeman.

boil one's head, (go away and) Dismissive expression.

boil over Become angry.

boiled shirt Stiff white shirt worn with tails.

boiling point, at About to become openly angry.

bollock* [v.] Reprimand severely. [n.] **bollocking**.

bollock-naked, (stark)* Naked. [Emph.]

bollocks*
1. Testicles.
2. Vulgar excl. (usu. of disagreement.)
3. Muddle. **make a bollocks of** Cause confusion. Bungle.
4. Nonsense.

boloney Nonsense. Rubbish.

bolshie (or-y) Stubbornly uncooperative.

bolt-hole Hiding place.

bomb
1. Large amount of money.
2. Cigarette containing drug.

bomb(shell)
1. Unexpected shock.
2. **drop a bomb(shell)** Cause a very unpleasant surprise.

bomb, like a Very quickly. Excellently, vigorously, very successful, etc.

bomb, make a Become very rich.

bonce Head.

bone [v.] Steal.

bone-head Simpleton. Also **bone-headed** Stupid.

bone-shaker Very old vehicle.

bone up (on) Study. Learn.

boner Mistake.

bonk [v.] Strike.

bonkers
1. Mad.
2. **stark staring bonkers** Entirely mad.

boob
1. Simpleton. Also **booby**.
2. See **boobs**.
3. [n.] & [v.] Blunder.

boobies See **boobs**.

booboo, make a Make a mistake.

boobs, boobies Female breasts.

book of words Instructions (in writing, but not necessarily in a book).

bookie Bookmaker.

boot
  1. **give the boot** Dismiss (usu. from employment).
  2. **boot out** Get rid of.
  3. **get the boot** Be dismissed (usu. from employment).
  4. **put the boot in** [Lit.] Kick. [Met.] Take decisive action (usu. to stop something).

boot-boy Youth affecting large boots.

boot-licker Sycophant.

boots See **bet one's boots**.

booze
  1. [n.] & [v.] Drink.
  2. **on the booze** Drinking heavily. Liable to drink heavily.
  3. **boozed(-up)** Intoxicated.

boozer
  1. One who is fond of drinking.
  2. Public house.

boozy [adj.] Drunken. (Usu. app. to function where plenty of alcoholic drink is available.)

bore the pants off one Bore one very considerably. Also **bore one rigid** *or* **stiff**.

born-days, in (all) one's Ever. [Emph.]

born yesterday, not Not young and foolish.

bosh Rubbish. Nonsense.

bosh-shot See **boss-shot**.

boss
  1. [n.] Head person. Chief. Owner. Manager. Any person in charge. Also **boss-man**.
  2. [v.] Exert the authority of **a boss**. Also **boss about** Nag with orders.
  3. [n.] Wife. [Facet.]
  4. [adj.] Principal. Chief.

boss-eyed Squinting. Crooked. Blind in one eye.

boss-shot Unsuccessful attempt. Guess.

bossy Over-inclined to be domineering.

bother Mild excl. of annoyance.

botheration Mild excl. of annoyance.

bottle Courage. Spirit. Also **bottle out** Show cowardice.

bottle, on the Drinking very heavily.

bottled Drunk.

bottle-washer Underling. Drudge.

bottom dollar See **bet one's boots**.

bottom drawer Place where girl keeps gifts, trousseau, etc., when preparing for marriage.

bottoms up! Good health! (Toast.)

bought it Suffered disaster or death.

bounce
1. Manhandle. Strike. Eject. Dismiss.
2. (Of cheque) Fail to be honoured by bank on which it is drawn.

bouncer Person employed to eject trouble-maker (e.g. from club).

bound, I'll be I'm sure. (Added to statement for emph.)

bounder Unpleasant, unreliable man.

bovver Stirring up of trouble (usu. quarrel or fight).

bovver-boots Large boots worn by **bovver boys**.

bovver boys Gangs of young hooligans affecting characteristic garb.

bowled out, be Be overcome or overwhelmed (e.g. be unable to answer a question). (From cricket, when a side is rapidly dismissed.)

bowler-hatted Compulsorily but honourably retired from commission in armed forces.

bow-wow Dog. [Juv.]

box
1. Television. **on the box** Appearing on TV.
2. Penalty-area (penalty-box) in football.

box clever [v.] Display intelligence or care.

box of tricks Any object having contents. Also similar to **bag of tricks**.

boyo Boy.

boys, the Group of men friends.

boys, one of the Associated with lively group of (usu. young) men friends.

bracelets Handcuffs.

bracer Pick-me-up.

bracket Nose. See also **punch up the bracket**.

brain Clever person. See also **brawn**.

brain-child Invention. Idea.

brain-drain Emigration of well-qualified people.

brainstorm Same as **brainwave** but usu. more lengthy and surprising.

brainwave Brilliant idea or sudden inspiration.

brash Cheeky. Self-assertive in vulgar way.

brass
1. Money.
2. Impudence. Also **brass neck**.

brass farthing
1. Coin of smallest value.
2. **not care** *or* **give a brass farthing** Not care in the slightest.

brass hat Senior officer in armed services. Also same as **top brass**.

brass-monkey weather
1. Extremely cold weather.
2.* **cold enough to freeze the balls off a brass monkey** Very cold.

brass neck Shameless impudence.

brass tacks
1. The essential facts.
2. **get down to brass tacks** Consider the basic practicalities as distinct from general theorising.

brassed off Bored and/or irritated.

brawn, brain before Intelligence is better than physical strength.

bread Money. Food.

bread-and-butter letter Letter of thanks to host/hostess after entertainment.

bread and scrape Bread thinly spread with butter, margarine, etc.

bread-basket Stomach.

bread is buttered, know which side one's Know what to do to retain or gain good fortune.

break
1. [n.] A piece of good fortune. Usu. **get a break**.
2. **give someone a break** Give someone opportunity to experience good fortune.
3. [n.] Interval. The period given over to advertisements during a TV programme.
4. [v.] Happen. Begin. Usu. journalese.
   • *The story broke three days ago.*

break it gently Tell unpleasant news in a way calculated to avoid pain.

break it up! Stop it! Don't do that! Disperse!

break one's back Work hard.

break one's neck Hurry.

breathe again Experience relief after a period of strain.

breathe down one's neck [Lit.] Pursue one. Be close to one.
[Met.] Supervise one closely, or ask frequently, e.g. with view to getting something done.

breeze in Enter briskly and casually.

breeze up, have the Be or become frightened.

brekker Breakfast.

brew up Make tea.

brick
1. Thoroughly dependable and kind person.
2. See **drop a brick** and **ton of bricks**.

brick wall, run one's head into Meet with insurmountable difficulties, opposition, etc. Attempt the impossible.

bricky Brick-layer.

briefs Men's underpants (or shorts).

bright and early In good time.

bright spark Fine or clever fellow. (Usu. ironical.)

bright specimen Foolish fellow.

brill Very enjoyable.

bring home the bacon Succeed in an undertaking. Earn sufficient to live.

bring off* Cause to experience sexual orgasm.

bring the house down Elicit great applause or laughter in a performance.

brinkmanship Daring (i.e. dangerous practice of seeing how far one can go).

briny, the The sea.

bristols Female breasts.

Brits British people.

broad
1. Unattached girl.
2. Prostitute.

broad as it's long, it's as It makes no difference.

broad in the beam Having large buttocks, hips, etc.

broke (to the wide or **world)** Penniless.

broke, go for Risk everything.

brolly Umbrella.

broth of a boy Fine fellow.

brothel creepers Shoes (usu. suede) with thick crepe soles.

brother
1. Friendly or comradely term of address.
2. Mild excl. of surprise or delight.

brown-hatter Male homosexual.

brown job Soldier.

browned off Utterly bored or depressed.

bruiser Boxer.

Brum(magem) Birmingham. Also **Brummie** Person from Birmingham.

brunch Combination of breakfast and lunch.

brush-off
1. Refusal. Snub.
2. **get the brush off** Fail to find favour. Be rebuffed.

Brussels sprouts Boy Scouts. [RS]

bubble and squeak Cold meat, potatoes and vegetables fried together.

bubbly Champagne.

buck
1. Dollar. Also **a fast buck** Money quickly earned.
2. Responsibility.
3. **pass the buck** Shift responsibility to someone else.
4. **the buck stops here** Mine is the ultimate responsibility.
5. **buck-passing** [n.] Shifting responsibility.

Buck house Buckingham Palace.

buck nigger Large male Negro. [Derog.]

buck up
1. Become more cheerful.
2. Hurry.

bucked Cheered. Made happy.

bucket down [v.] Rain heavily.

bucket, kick the Die.

bucketsful, raining or **coming down (in)** Raining very heavily.

buckshee Free of charge.

buddy
1. Close friend.
2. Term of address. [USA]

buff Devotee.

buff, the
1. Bare skin.
2. **in the buff** Naked.
3. **strip to the buff** Take off one's clothes.

buffer Elderly man, often incompetent or old-fashioned. (Usu. used with friendly contempt.)

bug
1. Irritate.
2. Fit secret listening-devices to a telephone, room, etc. Hence [n.] **bugging**.
3. **big bug** Important person.
4. [n.] Concealed listening device.
5. Defect.
6. Micro-organism, esp. one causing illness.

bug-bag Sleeping bag (as used in camping, etc.).

bug-house Cheap and/or shoddy cinema. Also **flea-pit**.

bug-hunter Entomologist.

bug-rake [n.] Comb.

bugger*
1. [n.] Unpleasant person or thing. Usu. offensive or contemptuous term app. to person. In certain contexts, can be quite amiable (see **bastard 2**).
2. [v.] Spoil. Also **bugger up** Bungle.
3. Strong excl. of surprise, disgust, etc. Also **bugger it, me**, etc.
4. Used in numerous expressions for emph.
    - *I'll be buggered*, I'm surprised.
    - *I'll be buggered if I'll do it*, I refuse to do it.
    - *I don't give a bugger*, I don't care in the least.
    - *Buggered if I know*, I don't know.

bugger about* Behave in desultory or feeble manner.

bugger all* Nothing.

bugger off* Depart.

buggeration* Same as **buggery**.

buggerlugs* Form of address (usu. offensive).

buggery* Used in several abusive expressions for emph.
- *Will I buggery!* I won't.
- *Go to buggery,* Go away.
- *It's all to buggery,* It is spoiled or confused.

Buggins' turn Turn, chance, opportunity, of the next person in line irrespective of merit (e.g. as in 'old boy' networks, election of mayors, etc.).

build-up
1. [n.] Advance preparation or publicity for an event (often with sense of increasing excitement). Flattery given to one when introducing one.
2. [v.] **build up** Arrange or offer this.

bulge Temporary increase in national birth-rate.

bull
1. See **bull(sh)**.
2. **bull up** Smarten.

bull at a gate, like a Vigorously. Wildly.

bull in a china shop Clumsy person.

bull point Point of superiority.

bull-shit Same as **bull(sh)**.

bull-shitter Glib person.

bull's eye Type of sticky sweet.

bulldog breed, spirit etc. Innate capacity for courage, endurance, toughness, peculiar to the English.

bulldoze Coerce. Succeed by overriding the opposition, e.g. in executing a plan or policy.

bull(sh)
1. Excessive attention to detail, esp. in cleaning military premises.
2. Nonsense.

bullet, get the
1. Be dismissed.
2. **give the bullet** Dismiss.

bullet-proof [adj.] Immune. Innocent. Protected.

bully for you! Well done!

bully rag [n.] & [v.] Bully.

bulsh See **bull(sh)**.

bum
1. [n.] Posterior.
2. [n.] Tramp.
3. [v.] Travel around, living cheaply, or by begging. Beg. Loaf.
4. [adj.] False. Of poor quality. Inefficient. Useless. Unsatisfactory. Inaccurate.

bum-boy Sodomite.

bum-fodder
1. Toilet paper.
2. Paper. Paper-work. Bureaucratic dependence on forms, letters, written memoranda, etc.

bum rap Imprisonment on false charge.

bum-sucker Sycophantic person.

bum-sucking [n.] Sycophancy. [adj.] Toadying.

bum's rush, get the Be ejected (usu. from place of entertainment, etc.).

bumbledom Inefficient, pompous and foolish officialdom.

bumbler Blunderer.

bumbling Stupid, clumsy, incoherent.

bumf Abbr. **bum-fodder**.

bump into Meet accidentally.

bump off [v.] Murder.

bump up Increase (e.g. costs).

bumper
1. [adj.] Very large or so special.
2. **bumpers** Female breasts.

bun in the oven, have a Be pregnant.

bun-fight Tea-party.

bunch
1. Group. Gang.
2. **best of the bunch** Best of those available.

bunch of fives Fist.

bundle
1. [n.] & [v.] Fight.
2. **go** or **do a bundle on** Enjoy or support very enthusiastically.
3. **bundle of nerves, a** An extremely nervous or sensitive person.
4. Large sum of money.

bung
1. [v.] Throw vigorously.
2. [n.] Blow.

bung ho!
1. Good health! (Toast.)
2. Good-bye!

bung it in Put it in.

bung over Hand, pass over.
- *Bung over the jam, please.*

bung up
1. [v.] Close.
2. **bunged up** Blocked up.

bungaloid Having many bungalows. (Of landscape, etc.) Term of abuse applied to spread of housing over the countryside.
- *Bungaloid growth.*

bungy
1. Cheese.
2. Indiarubber.

bunk Nonsense.

bunk, do a Vanish. Hurry away quickly.

bunk off Play truant.

bunk-up, give one a Help one to climb up.

bunny-girl Hostess at night-club (usu., but not necessarily, dressed in brief costume with long ears and fluffy tail).

bunny-grub Fresh green vegetables (usu. in salad).

burg Town. City.

burk(e) See **berk**.

burn [n.] & [v.] Smoke. (Of cigarettes, etc.)

burn oneself out Become incapacitated by too much effort.

burn up (the road or **the miles)** Drive very fast (along the road or for miles).

burp [n.] & [v.] Belch.

burton, go for a Vanish. Become useless. Be killed or destroyed.

bus
1. **miss the bus** Lose the opportunity.
2. [n.] Car. Aeroplane. [Facet.]

bushed Tired out.

bush telegraph, by or **on the** By private, secret, informal or unofficial information or rumour.

business, do one's Defecate.

business end The end or part which is the effectively operating one.
- *He sat down on the business end of a drawing-pin.*

business, like nobody's In a remarkable way.

busk Sing or entertain in the streets to collect money. [n.] **busker** One who does this.

busman's holiday Person who spends his holiday doing that which he normally does for a living.

bust
1. Destroy.
2. Enter illegally.
3. Break. Broken.
4. Arrest.
5. Penniless. Bankrupt.

6. [n.] Police search or raid. [Pop.] Also [v.].

7. Burst.

8. **go bust** Fail to operate. (Of business) Fail to succeed.

bust-up Violent quarrel.

busted

1. Burst. Broken.

2. Arrested, following a police search for drugs. [Pop.]

buster

1. Tough, lively person.

2. Term of address, usu. aggressive.

busy, get Become active.

butch Aggressively *or* exceptionally masculine man (*or* woman).

butchers, have *or* **take a** Look.

butt Buttocks.

butter-fingers Clumsy person.

butter-up Flatter.

buttered on both sides, want one's bread Make unreasonable demand or request.

butterflies in the stomach Feelings of apprehension, nervousness, fear, etc.

butterfly mind Mind unable to concentrate on any one topic for a long time, before passing on to another.

button loose *or* **short, have a** Be mentally weak.

button one's lip Be silent.

buttoned up

1. Satisfactorily concluded.

2. Non-committal.

butty

1. Buttered bread. Sandwich.

2. Companion. Friend.

3. Intermediary between proprietors and workers in a business.

buy

1. Be deceived by.

2. Listen.
  • *Go on, I'll buy it*, I'll listen.
3. Accept. Believe.
  • *I won't buy that excuse.*
4. Incur something unpleasant. Similar to **ask for it**. See also **bought it**.

buy a pup Be swindled.

buy oneself out Purchase one's discharge from the armed forces.

buzz
1. [n.] Rumour.
2. [v.] Throw.
3. [v.] Call by telephone.
4. [n.] Telephone call.

buzz off Go away.

buzzer Telephone.

by a long chalk By a considerable amount.

by gum, jingo, jupiter, jove, etc. Mild excl.

by the board See **go by the board**.

by the short hairs, have one Have one at a disadvantage. Also **have one by the short and curlies**.

bye (-bye) Good-bye.

C

cabbage
1. [v.] Save. Steal. Retrieve. Make good. Get back.
   - *We'll take this short cut and cabbage a little time.*
2. [n.] Lifeless or unambitious person.

cabbage-head Simpleton.

cabbage-looking, I'm not so green as I'm I am not as foolish or inexperienced as you may imagine.

cabbage-patch Small garden.

cabby Taxi-driver.

caboodle, the (whole) The entire situation, collection of objects, etc.

cack-handed
1. Clumsy.
2. Left-handed.

cackle See **cut the cackle**.

cadge, be on the Be in a position of asking for something.

caff Café.

cagey Secretive. Cautious. [n.] **cageyness.**

cagmag Rubbish. Nonsense.

cahoots with, in In league with.

Cain, raise Become angry. Create a disturbance.

cake-hole Mouth.

cake, piece of Easy undertaking. Anything uncomplicated.

cake-walk (Unexpectedly) easy undertaking.

call-girl Prostitute (usu. contacted by telephone).

call it a day Consider something to be finished. End work for the day.

call it a deal Regard the matter as concluded. (Usu. applied to bargaining.)

call one everything under the sun Be comprehensively abusive to one.

call, pay a Go to the lavatory.

camp
    1. [adj.] Exaggerated. Affected. Effeminate.
    2. [adj.] Homosexual. Also **camp as a row of pink tents**.
    3. [v.] Behave in exaggerated and/or effeminate way. Usu. **camp it up** (often theat.).
    4. [n.] Behaviour of this kind. Also **high camp** Specially prominent behaviour of this kind.

can [n.] Prison.

can, carry the Bear the blame or responsibility.

can you beat it! Excl. of astonishment.

cancer stick Cigarette.

cane [v.]
    1. Treat harshly. Attack verbally.
    2. **get a caning** Be defeated or reprimanded. Be harshly treated. Also **get caned**.

canned
    1. Intoxicated.
    2. (Of music) Recorded.

canoodle Fondle or talk amorously. Flirt.

can't do that there 'ere, you You are not permitted to do that [Facet.].

caper [n.] Activity. Occupation.

card Attractively odd sort of person (usu. amusingly and unconsciously unconventional).

cards Employee's documents held by employer. Thus **get one's cards** be dismissed; **ask for one's cards** Ask to leave employment; **give someone his cards** Dismiss him.

care a brass farthing, a damn, a fig, a monkey's toss*, a rap, a tinker's cuss, not to Not to care in the slightest.

care, for all I I do not care.

care less See **couldn't care less**.

carpet [v.] Reprimand. [n.] **carpeting**.

carpet, on the About to be reprimanded.

carroty Red-haired.

carry on
1. Indulge in protracted grief, censure or anger.
2. Behave in foolish and/or flightly manner.

carry-on
1. Extraordinary activity or behaviour. Also plural **carryings-on**.
2. **what a carry-on!** Excl. at extraordinary event.

carry the banner Serve an ideal one believes in.

carry the can (back) Bear the responsibility or blame.

carsey Lavatory. Also **Kahsi**.

cart (away, etc.) Carry (away, etc.).

cart, in the In trouble or difficulty.

carve up
1. [v.] Cheat. Destroy. Defeat. Attack. Fight. Share out booty.

carve-up [n.] Swindle. Division and distribution of loot. Removal of person by underhand means.

case
1. [n.] Unusual person. See **hard case**.
2. [v.] Examine. Usu. **case a joint** Surreptitiously inspect a place (in preparation for robbing it). [n.] **Casing**.

cash in Take advantage of opportunity to make money.

cast-iron Irrefutable.

cast nasturtiums Cast aspersions.

cast-offs Discarded clothing.

cat
1. Spiteful woman.
2. Person [Pop.].

cat got your tongue, has the Why are you saying nothing?

cat in hell's chance, not to have a To have no chance.

cat jumps, see how *or* **which way the** Wait and see what happens.

cat laugh, enough to make a Amusing.

cat lick Brief wash.

cat on hot bricks, like a In a state of nervous tension.

cat's brought in, something the Disreputable-looking person or thing.

cat's pyjamas *or* **whiskers, the** Supremely good.

catch bending Confront when at a disadvantage.

catch it Be reprimanded or punished.

catch on
1. Become popular.
2. Understand.

catch on the hop Surprise.

catch one's death (of cold) Get a (severe) chill.

catch 22 Position in which one cannot win, whatever one does.

catch with one's trousers down Confront when at a disadvantage.

caught See **catch**.

caught short Caught at a disadvantage. Needing to go to the lavatory.

caution Unusual person, usu. amusing.

cavort Prance.

cert
1. Certainty.
2. **dead cert** Something which is sure to happen.

chair-borne In an administrative capacity.

chalk, by a long By very much.

chalk up Make a favourable note of. Regard as favourable.

champ Abbr. Champion.

champion [adj.] Excellent. Also excl. of pleasure.

chance
1. [v.] Risk.
2. **chance it** Take a risk.
3. **chance one's arm** *or* **luck** Take a risk.
4. **Chance would be a fine thing** There's not much chance of that [Facet. reply].

change Satisfaction. Assistance.
- *I got no change out of him.* He refused to help me.

chap(py) Man. Boy.

char
1. Tea.
2. [Abbr.] Charwoman.
3. [v.] Do cleaning work in office, house, etc.

character
1. Odd person.
2. Interesting, lively person.

charlie *or* **-y**
1. Mildly foolish person.
2. **a right** *or* **proper Charlie** Very foolish.

charts, in the (Of popular music) Achieving the success of being among the most frequently sold gramophone records.

chase Try to reach (usu. target).

chase the dragon Inhale heroin fumes.

chase (up) Hasten a piece of work, or the person doing it.

chase yourself, (go and) Go away.

chaser A second drink to follow the first (usu. spirits following, or alternating with, beer).

chat up Initiate polite conversation with (usu. for a specific purpose, often to make overtures to a lady).

cheap at half the price Expensive.

cheap, feel Feel ashamed (usu. of oneself).

check! Correct!

check out Confirm. Examine with a view to confirming.

check out with Agree with. Conform to.

Cheddar, hard! Bad luck!

cheeks Buttocks.

cheep, not a Not a sound. No response.

cheerio
1. Good-bye.
2. Good luck! (Toast).

cheers!
1. Same as **cheerio**.
2. Thank you.

cheery-bye Good-bye.

cheese, big Important person.

cheese-cake Feminine charm (usu. on provocative display).

cheese, hard! Bad luck!

cheese it! Stop!

cheesed (off) Bored. Disgruntled.

chemmy Chemin-de-fer. (Game)

chest, get something off one's Say something to relieve's one feelings.

chesty Having a troublesome chest illness.

chew the fat *or* **rag** Grumble. Complain. Argue. Discuss.

chew over Consider (at leisure).

chew up Reprimand. Annoy.

chewed up
1. Exhausted.
2. Annoyed.
3. Reprimanded.

chick
1. Young woman.
2. Affectionate term of address to child.
3. Girl-friend.

chicken
1. [n.] Coward. Children's game involving challenges.
2. [adj.] Cowardly.
3. **no chicken** Elderly.
4. **chicken-hearted** Cowardly.

chicken-feed A trivial sum or matter, not enough to be worth consideration.

chicken out Retire or fail to appear (usu. when at risk).

chief cook See **head cook**.

chi-ike
1. Make uproar. (Various spellings.)
2. Behave impertinently. Barrack.

chimp [Abbr.] Chimpanzee.

chin-chin! Good luck! (Toast.)

chin up! Be courageous and cheerful.

china Mate or chum.

China, not for all the tea in On no account.

Chink Chinaman [derog.].

chinwag [n.] & [v.] Gossip. Talk.

chip in
1. Interrupt.
2. Subscribe money.

chippy
1. Fish-and-chip shop.
2. Carpenter.

chips are down, the One has accepted a risk, taken a gamble, committed oneself to a course of action.

chips, have (had) one's
1. Die.
2. Fail to succeed. Be finished.

chirpy Lively.

chisel [v.] Cheat. Swindle.

chiseller Swindler.

chivvy Chase. Hustle. Encourage. Keep up to the mark. Also **chivvy along** *or* **up**.

chiz Cheat. Swindle. Usu. excl. of annoyance.

choc-ice Ice cream encased in chocolate.

chock-a-block Absolutely full. Also **chockablock**.

chocker
  1. Disgruntled.
  2. [Abbr.] **chockablock**.

choke Become upset usu. to point of speechlessness or tears.

choke off Rebuff. Dismiss. Reprimand.

choked (-off), be Be disgruntled or upset.

chok(e)y Prison.

choosey Difficult to please.

chop
  1. [v.] Cancel. Delete. Cut out.
  2. **get the chop** Be cut, curtailed, dismissed, eliminated.
  3. **chops** Mouth.

chop-chop! Quickly!

chopper
  1. Helicopter.
  2. Penis.
  3. **choppers** Teeth.

chow
  1. [n.] Food.
  2. Expression of greeting. (From Italian.) Properly **ciao**.

chronic Severe. Very tiresome. Disagreeable.

chuck [v.]
  1. Throw.
  2. **chuck in** *or* **up** Cease. Abandon.
  3. **chuck up** Stop doing it.

chuck, get the Be dismissed from employment.

chuck one's hand in Abandon as hopeless.

chuck one's weight about Assert oneself or one's authority aggressively.

chuck out Throw away. Eject.

chuck over Abruptly end a partnership or friendship with.

chuck up the sponge Surrender. Give up.

chucker-out Person employed to eject unwanted people from places of entertainment.

chucking-out time Closing-time at public house, etc.

chucklehead Simpleton.

chuffed Pleased.

chum Special friend.

chum up with Make friends with.

chummy Friendly.

chump
   1. Foolish person.
   2. **off one's chump** Slightly unhinged.

chunk Thick piece (of meat, wood, etc.).

chunky Thick.

Chunnel Tunnel beneath the English Channel.

churchyard cough Persistent, rasping cough.

cig(gy) Cigarette.

cinch
   1. Certainty.
   2. Something very easy to accomplish.

circs Circumstances.

circus Group of sportsmen (e.g. tennis players) competing against each other on tour.

cissy Effeminate person. (Usu. juv. term of contempt for boy supposed to lack manly qualities.)

civvies Civilian clothes, as opposed to service uniform.

civvy street Civilian life, as opposed to life in armed forces.

clag Dirt.

clam up [v.] Become silent.

clanger
1. [n.] Blunder.
2. **drop a clanger** Make a serious mistake.

clap Gonorrhoea.

clapped out Worn out. Exhausted.

clappers, like the (merry) Very quickly or vigorously.

class High quality. [adj.] **classy** Superior.

clatter [v.] Strike (person).

claw back Retrieve (usu. of money to be recovered in the course of business).

claws, in one's In one's power.

clean Without impropriety.

clean, come Confess everything.

clean job of it, make a Do thoroughly.

clean, keep it Allow no impropriety to intrude.

clean out Take everything away, usu. money (by theft).

clean up
1. Gain money.
2. Improve by a systematic campaign. [n.] **clean-up.**

clean round the bend Quite mad.

cleaned out Penniless.

cleaners, take to the Defeat heavily.

clear as mud Incomprehensible.

clear, in the Innocent.

cleavage Hollow between woman's breasts, usu. as seen when low-cut dress is worn.

clem
1. Starve.
2. [adj.] **clemmed** Very hungry.

clever clogs *or* **dick** Know-all.

click
1. Have a piece of good luck, esp. in establishing relationships (with opposite sex).
2. Make sense (usu. suddenly).

clinch [n.] Embrace.

clink [n.] Prison.

clip
1. [v.] Strike a smart blow. Usu. **clip one's ear**.
2. **at a good clip** At a fast speed.

clip-joint Unjustifiably expensive place of entertainment (usu. restaurant or night-club).

clobber
1. [n.] Clothes. Possessions. Also any collection of objects.
2. [v.] Strike. Reprimand. Remind. Check. Cause to stop (usu. with view to punishment).
   • *She was clobbered for speeding.*

clobbering, get a Suffer defeat, set-back, harsh reprimand or punishment.

clock [v.]
1. Measure time or speed (e.g. of person running a race).
2. Spend (a measured amount of time).
   • *The winner clocked seven minutes.*
3. [n.] Face.
4. [v.] Hit.
5. **clock up** Attain.

clonk Hit.

close call, shave *or* **thing** Narrow escape.

clot Fool.

cloth ears, have
1. Be inattentive. Fail to hear something.
2. **cloth ears** Form of address to inattentive person.

clothes-line, be able to sleep on a Be very tired.

cloud seven *or* **nine, on** Very happy.

clout
1. [n.] Heavy blow.
2. [v.] Strike heavy blow.
3. [n.] Influence.

club, (put) in the (pudding) (Make) pregnant.

cluck, dumb Foolish person. Simpleton.

clue, not have a
1. Have no idea.
2. Also comprehensively dismissive expression.
   • *He hasn't a clue*, He is totally incompetent.

clue in *or* **up** Inform.

clued-up, clued-in [adj.] Well-informed, well-prepared, efficient.

clueless Irresponsible. Vague. Ignorant.

clumping Clumsy.

cobble Patch up. Also **cobble together** Fabricate (usu. roughly).

cobblers
1. Testicles.
2. Nonsense. Also **a load of cobblers** (Quite polite usage, despite 1).
3. **cobblers!** Excl. of disagreement.

cobs off, knock Defeat easily. Exhaust.

cock
1. Penis.
2. Nonsense. Also **a load of cock** (but less polite than **cobblers**).
3. Affectionate term of address. Also **old cock(-sparrow)**.
4. **all to cock** [adj.] Bungled. In a state of confusion.

cock a snook Show derision or contempt.

cock-eyed Irregular. Bungled. Inaccurate. Awry. Squinting.

cock-fighting, beat Be extremely enjoyable, surprising or exciting.

cock-teaser* Woman who tries to excite one sexually but stops short of sexual intercourse.

cock up [v.] Bungle.
- *He tried to do it himself, but he cocked it up.*

cock-up [n.] Blunder, succession of blunders, or the consequence of these.

cocoa, I should I don't care.

cod Deceive. Hoodwink.

codger Old man.

codswallop Nonsense.

co-ed Co-educational.

coffin-nail Cigarette.

coke
1. Coca-cola.
2. Cocaine.
3. **Go and eat coke** Go away.

cold
1. **leave one cold** Fail to move or impress one.
2. See **knock cold** and **brass-monkey**.
3. **have cold** Have at one's mercy.
4. [adj.] Unconscious. Usu. **out cold**.

cold feet
1. Anxiety. Cowardice.
2. **get cold feet** Become fearful.

cold storage, in Deferred for later consideration.

cold turkey, go Deny oneself narcotics.

collar [v.] Appropriate.

collect Meet (a person) to accompany or take him elsewhere.

collywobbles
1. Pain in the stomach.
2. Feelings of apprehension.

Colonel Blimp See **Blimp**.

colour of one's money, see the See, or have proof of existence of, one's actual cash, as distinct from promises to pay.

column, dodge the Avoid work.

combo Group of instrumentalists usu. pop. or jazz.

come
1. [v.] Experience sexual orgasm. Also **come off**.
2. [n.] Semen.
3. **come it** Same as **come the acid**.

come a cropper Fall heavily. Fail badly.

come across Project oneself.
- *He comes across very badly on TV.*

come again! Please repeat what you have just said.

come-back Reaction. Response. Retort. Retaliation.

come clean Confess everything.

come-down Humiliation. Anti-climax. Less pleasing or satisfactory position than previously.

come down like a ton of bricks See **like a ton** . . .

come good Succeed.

come it
1. Behave ostentatiously, to impress.
2. Deceive. Behave deceitfully.

come it over *or* **with** Get the better of. Impress. Deceive.

come it (strong) Exaggerate. Show vigour.

come off
1. Experience sexual orgasm. 2. Succeed.

come off it! You can't expect me to believe that!

come on! Same as **come off it!**

come-on [n.] Humorous piece of trickery. Lure.

come out of the ark Be very old.

come out strong Behave vigorously or impressively (usu. **against**).

come over
1. Affect temporarily.
   - *Something came over me,* I felt ill.
2. Impose on.
3. Same as **come it over**.

come the acid
1. Behave overbearingly, or unpleasantly. Exaggerate.
2. Transfer one's responsibility to another person.
3. Be sarcastic.

come the old soldier Impress by claiming superior experience or wisdom.

come to that Since you mention it.

come to think of it When one considers.

come undone *or* **unstuck** Fail. Go wrong.

comeuppance, get one's Receive one's deserts. Meet ultimate disaster.

comfy Comfortable.

comic
1. Children's periodical.
2. Professional comedian.

coming or going, not to know if one is Be flustered, confused.

coming, see one Realise one's innocence or gullibility, and take advantage of it.

coming to one, have it Is likely to suffer for present actions.

common [Abbr.] Common sense.

common or garden Commonplace.

con
1. [n.] Swindle. Deception.
2. [n.] Deceitful person.
3. **con game** Trick to obtain money from the credulous.
4. **con man** Trickster (usu. of persuasive tongue).
5. [v.] Trick. Swindle.

concern [n.] Thing.

conchie Conscientious objector to compulsory enrolment in armed forces.

confab *or* **conflab** Discussion.

confound it! Excl. of annoyance.

confounded Inconvenient. Unpleasant. Excessive.

conk Nose.

conk out Break down completely (usu. of machinery). Die.

contraption Any kind of device (usu. mechanical).

coo! Excl. of surprise.

cook
1. Falsify (usu. applied to financial accounts).
2. **cook the books** Falsify the account-books.

cooking, what's What's being planned?

cookie
1. Person.
2. **that's the way the cookie crumbles** That is how things are.
3. **see which way the cookie crumbles** See what happens.

cooking
1. [v.] Happening. About to happen.
2. [n.] Cheap draught-beer.

cool
1. Pleasing. [Pop.]
2. **(real) cool** (Very) self-possessed. In the fashion, but not wildly or eccentrically so. [Pop.]
3. See **keep one's cool**.
4. Emph. adj. (with sums of money only, e.g.
   • *a cool hundred*, one hundred pounds).
5. **play it cool** Act moderately.

cool cat
1. Person interested in jazz.
2. Fine fellow.

cool it [v.] Cause it (i.e. matters) to become calmer or more cautious.

cooler Cell. Prison.

coot
1. Simpleton.
2. See **bald as a coot**.

cop
1. [v.] Catch. Capture.
2. [n.] Policeman.

3. [n.] Capture. Arrest.

4. **not much cop** Not very good. Of little use or value. Also **no cop**.

cop it Get into trouble. Be punished. Die.

cop out [v.] Abandon. Similar to **opt out** Usu. **cop out of** Cease to be interested in or committed to. Escape. Fail to take action, out of fear.

cop-out [n.] Betrayal of principles. Evasion. Loss of nerve. Cowardice.

cop-shop Police station.

copper
1. Policeman.
2. **copper's nark** Criminal who cooperates with police (usu. by informing).
3. **copper-nob** Red-haired person.

copy-cat Person who imitates another.

cor (lumme or **stone the crows)!** Excl. of surprise or disgust.

corker Remarkably excellent person or thing.

corking First-rate.

corn
1. That which is hackneyed, and usu. sentimental. (Of films, books, etc.)
2. **earn one's corn** Earn one's keep.

corner, just around the Imminent.

corny Out-of-date. Hackneyed. Stale. Sentimental.

corporation Protruding stomach.

corpse [v.] Make a mistake, while acting a part on the stage (usu. by laughing unintentionally).

cosh
1. [n.] Short, heavy stick.
2. [v.] Strike with **cosh**.

cosh, under the (Of people) under pressure. Put into a state of tension.

cost a packet Be very expensive.

cotton on (to)
1. Understand.
2. Have a liking for.
3. Attach oneself to.

cough Confess.

cough up
1. Pay. Produce. Hand over.
2. Disclose.

could be [Abbr.] It might possibly be so.

could eat the hind legs off a donkey, I I am very hungry.

couldn't care less, I I do not care at all.

count (person) out Exclude him.

couth Cultured; refined; sophisticated. (Facet. opp. of 'un-couth'.)

cove Chap. Fellow.

cover up for one Help one by concealing or rectifying one's mistakes.

cow Unpleasant woman.

cowboy Casual worker, usu. unskilled or unscrupulous.

cow-juice Milk.

cows come home, till the Indefinitely.

coward(l)y custard Coward. [Juv.]

crack
1. [n.] Witty retort. Joke.
2. [adj.] First-class. Expert.
3. [v.] Break open. Also **crack a bottle** Open a bottle (of wine) and drink.
4. **have a crack** Make an attempt.
5. [v.] Solve.

crack down on Suppress. Reduce.

crack of dawn Daybreak.

crack of the whip, (fair) Fair chance.

crack on (*or* along)
1. Move ahead (quickly).
2. Pretend.

crack-pot
1. [n.] Crazy person.
2. [adj.] Crazy. Impracticable.

crack-up
1. Praise.
   - *It's not all that it's cracked up to be.* It's not as good as people claim.
2. Break down. Also [n.] **crack-up**.

cracked Crazy.

cracker Person or thing having remarkably pleasing qualities.

crackers Mad.

cracking [adj.]
1. Fast.
   - *A cracking pace.*
2. Excellent.
3. **get cracking** Start.

crackling, a (nice) bit of Attractive woman.

cradle-snatcher Same as **baby-snatcher**.

cramp one's style Curtail or impede one's efforts or progress. Handicap one.

crap*
1. [n.] Defecation.
2. Anything worthless, objectionable etc. [adj.] **crappy.**
3. [v.] Defecate. Also **have a crap**.

crash Fail badly.

crash a party [v.] Join a party uninvited. Also **crash in, gate-crash**.

crash bag Bed.

crash pad Place for casual sleepers. [Pop.]

crash out
1. Go to sleep (usu. in someone else's house, or uninvited, e.g. at a party).
2. End an experience of taking the drug LSD. [Pop.]

crashing bore Extremely boring person or thing.

crate Old vehicle (usu. car or aircraft).

crawl
1. Behave obsequiously, sycophantically.
2. [n.] **crawler** One who does this.

crawling Covered with lice or other vermin. Thronged with (people).

crazy
1. Extremely exciting, usu. unrestrainedly.
2. (with **about** etc.) Very enthusiastic.
3. **crazy mixed-up (kid)** Psychologically disturbed (youngster).
4. **like crazy** Like mad.

crease
1. Amuse exceedingly.
2. [adj.] **creased** Very amused.
3. Exhaust. Tire out.

create Make a fuss.

creek, up the
1. In difficulties.
2. Crazy.

creep, creeper
1. Same as **crawl, crawler**, with additional suggestion of slyness.
2. **creep** [n.] Any unpleasant person.
3. **creeping Jesus** Obsequious person.

creeps, the Sensations of fear, horror, revulsion.

crib
1. [n.] Book giving answers to problems, translations, etc., e.g. at school.
2. **cribber** One who uses **crib**.

cricket, not Not fair.

crikey! Mild excl. of surprise.

croak Die.

crock
1. Person or thing incapacitated by age or infirmity.
2. **old crock** Old car.

crocked Damaged. Injured.

crocodile Line of people walking (usu. in pairs).

crook Criminal. Rogue.

cropper Heavy fall. See **come a cropper**.

cross Cheat.

cross (as two sticks) Bad-tempered.

cross my heart (and hope to die)! I swear I am speaking the truth.

crown [v.] Hit over the head.

crud Detestable person.

cruddy Nasty.

crumbs! Mild excl. of surprise.

crummy Of poor quality.

crumpet Sexually attractive woman or women. Female sexual attractiveness in general.
● *A nice bit of crumpet.* An attractive woman.

crunch [n.] Test (usu. test of strength between two forces). Often **when it comes to the crunch** *or* **when the crunch comes**. When the most important test occurs.

crush
1. Sentimental passion (usu. on part of an adolescent) for another person.
2. **have a crush on** Be infatuated with.

cry all the way to the bank Make a lot of money despite being criticised.

crying out loud, for Excl. of exasperation.

cuckoo
1. Crazy person.
2. Term of address (usu. mixture of affection and reproach).
3. [adj.] Crazy.

cuffs Handcuffs.

culture vulture Person exceptionally keen on the arts.

cunt*
    1. Female private parts. Hence, sexual intercourse. Also as **crumpet**, but much more vulgar.
    2. Objectionable person. Also term of address.
        • *You silly cunt.*

cup of tea What is congenial or desired.

cuppa *or* **cupper** Cup of tea.

curate's egg, like the Part good, part bad. Usu. **good in parts, like the curate's egg**.

curlies, have one by the short and Have one at a disadvantage.

curse, not worth a Worthless.

curse, the Menstruation.

curtains The end.

cushy Easy. Pleasant.

cuss
    1. Curse.
    2. Person (usu. one who is **cussed**).

cussed Perverse. Obstinate. [n.] **cussedness**.

customer
    1. Person with whom one has dealings e.g. **awkward** *or* **queer customer**.
    2. **cool customer** Person displaying effrontery or self-possession.
    3. **ugly customer** Difficult person to handle.

cut
    1. [v.] Ignore. Absent oneself from.
    2. [v.] Excise.
    3. [v.] Move quickly. Also **cut along**.
    4. **cut and run** Leave hastily.
    5. **cut dead** Refuse to acknowledge (a person).
    6. [adj.] Drunk. Also **half-cut**.
    7. [n.] Share (usu. of commission or profits).

cut a figure Make an impression.

cut above, a Slightly above. Of a higher standard than. A degree beyond (one's means, one's level, etc.).

cut down to size Lower (a person's estimate of his own importance) to a realistic level.

cut it out Stop it. Be quiet.

cut no ice Convince no-one. Make no difference.

cut out Suited.
- *He's not cut out for the job.*

cut that! Stop doing or saying that!

cut the cackle! Be quiet! Come to the point!

cut the cackle and come to the 'osses *or* **horses** Get down to business. Leave out the non-essentials and come to the part that matters.

cut-throat
1. Reduced to minimum of profit.
   - *The goods are at cut-throat prices.*
2. Intensely competitive.

cut up nasty *or* **ugly** *or* **rough** Become quarrelsome, angry or offensive.

cute Attractive. Ingenious. [n.] **cutie** Attractive girl.

D

DJ
  1. One who introduces and plays gramophone records on the radio, etc. [Abbr.] Disc-jockey.
  2. [Abbr.] Dinner jacket.

DTs Acute form of delirium brought on by heavy drinking. [Abbr.] Delirium tremens.

dab(-hand) Expert.

dabs Fingerprints.

dad *or* **daddio** Term of address to older man. (Facet.)

daddy of them all Best of its type.

daffy Stupid.

daft as a brush Very silly.

dago Person from Mediterranean country, esp. Spain and Italy (not France), usually slightly dark-skinned. [Derog.]

daily Domestic worker who comes every day.

daily dozen Daily physical exercises.

daisy chain Homosexual clique.

damage Cost. Expense.

dame Young woman.

damn
  1. Excl. or mild curse.
  2. Negligible amount, as in **not worth a damn** *or* **not care** *or* **give a (tuppenny) damn**.
  3. [adj.] or [adv.] Same as **damned**.

damn all Nothing.

damn it, dammit! Mild excl.

damn it (or **dammit), as near as** Very near.
  • *He came as near as dammit to scoring.*

damn(ed) near [adv.] Almost.

damn(ed) thing, a Anything.

damn(ed) well Certainly.

damned
  1. Adj. or adv. of emph., expressing irritation but little meaning.
    • *I'll be damned if I'll do it.* I won't do it.
  2. **I'll be damned** Excl. of surprise.
  3. **damned if I know** I don't know.

dander
  1. Anger. Irritation.
  2. **have one's dander up** Be angry.

damper on, put the Discourage.

dandy Pleasing. See **fine and dandy**.

dark Unused (of theatres).

darn(ed) Evasion of **damn(ed)**.

dash (it) (it all)! Excl. of mild annoyance.

dashed Evasion of **damned**.

date
  1. [n.] Appointment to meet someone (often of opp. sex).
  2. [n.] Person whom one has an appointment to meet for social purposes.
  3. [v.] Make such an appointment.

day, that'll be the Rueful or sardonic comment expressing disbelief in the likelihood of a piece of good fortune just referred to.

daylight robbery Extortionate charge or cost.

daylights out of, knock or **beat the (living)** Thrash. Overwhelm. Overcome. Defeat heavily. Also **frighten** or **scare** (etc.) **the (living) daylights out of** Frighten considerably.

dead
1. Empty. (Of glasses, bottles, etc.).
2. Extremely. Completely.
   - *Dead lucky.*

dead-and-alive Dull. Unexciting.

dead as mutton Dead. [Emph.] Finished. Obsolete.

dead beat
1. [n.] Lazy person.
2. [adj.] Exhausted.

dead cert See **cert**.

dead duck A matter (e.g. idea, controversy, prospect) which is at an end.

dead from the neck upwards Stupid.

dead head Stupid person.

dead in it, wouldn't be seen Refuse to have anything to do with it.

dead loss Useless thing or person. Waste of time.

dead nuts on Extremely interested in or attached to.

dead on Very accurate.

dead-pan Expressionless.

dead set
1. Determined.
2. **make a dead set at** Make a determined attempt at.
3. **be dead set** Be very determined.

dead spit of, the Exactly like.

dead trouble, in In serious trouble.

dead with, wouldn't be seen Refuse to have anything to do with.

deal, do a Make a bargain.

deal! It's a I agree to what is proposed.

dear(ie)(y) Form of affectionate address.

death Unbearable.
- *The whole function's going to be death.*

death (warmed-up), like Sickly, feeble, lifeless.

de-bag Remove the trousers of.

debrief Obtain information from, after an event. **be debriefed** Undergo questioning after an event. (Usu. military).

debunk Remove glamour or tradition (from institution, cult, person, etc.) by plain speaking.

deck Floor. Ground.

Dee-Jay Same as **DJ**.

deep Cunning. Secretive.

deep end, go (in) off the Become angrily excited.

dekko [n.] Glance; look.

deliver the goods Do what is expected or required.

demo Demonstration.

demon [n.] & [adj.] Expert.

depends, it all Perhaps.

desert rats Eighth Army [WWII].

deuce
1. Evasion of **devil**.
   - *What the deuce are we to do?*
2. **the deuce to pay** Trouble. Serious consequences.

deuced Very.

devil for . . . , a One who much enoys . . .

devil of a . . . , a Emph. addition to sentence.
   - *They were making a devil of a noise.* They were being extremely noisy.

devil, the
1. Emph. addition after numerous words, e.g. why, what, who, where, how, etc.
   - *(What the devil are you doing?)* expressing surprise, irritation, etc.
2. **play the devil with** Damage. Upset. Harm.

devil's own, the Extremely difficult.
   - *It'll be the devil's own job to persuade him.*

dex(ies) Amphetamine drug tablets.

dhobying Washing of clothes.

diabolical Unacceptable.

dial Face (of person).

dibs Money.

dice, no No prospect.

dicey Risky. Uncertain.

dick
1. Penis.
2. Policeman. Detective.

dickens, the Same as **the devil**.

dick(e)y *or* **-ie**
1. Unwell. **dicky heart** Weak heart.
2. Detachable, starched shirt-front.
3. Risky. Tricky. Unsound.

dicky-bird Bird [Juv.]

dicky-bird, not a Nothing.

did you ever? Did you ever hear of, see, etc., such a thing before?

diddies Female breasts.

diddle Cheat.

diddler Swindler.

diddy Little.

dig
1. [v.] Live in lodgings.
2. [n.] Archaeological excavation.
3. [v.] Enjoy. Understand. Admire.

dig in Begin eating heartily.

dig out *or* **up** Search for and find.

digs Lodgings.

digger [n.] Australian.

dilly-dally Loiter. Vacillate.

dim
1. Stupid. Slow.
2. Unimportant.
   - *A rather dim public school.*
3. **dim wit** Foolish person.
4. **dim-witted** Stupid.

dim view of, take a Object to.

dimbo Slow-witted person.

din-dins Dinner. [Juv.]

ding-dong
1. [n.] Quarrel. Lively argument.
2. [adj.] Vigorous.

dinkum, (fair) Good.

dinky Dainty. Pleasant. Neat.

dip
1. [v.] Fail (an exam.).
2. [n.] Bathe.
3. [n.] Pick-pocket.

dip one's wick (Of men) Have sexual intercourse.

dippy Slightly mad.

dipso Dipsomaniac. Very heavy drinker.

dirt
1. Information.
2. Scandalous gossip.
3. **throw dirt** Be malicious.

dirty
1. Emph. adv. Very.
   - *Dirty big hole.* Very large hole.
2. **do the dirty** Perform a mean action.

dirty end of the stick, get the Find oneself coping with the unpleasant aspect of a matter, or the worst of a bargain.

dirty great Very considerable.

dirty look Unfriendly or hostile look.

dirty old men (in mackintoshes) Sexually obsessed middle-aged or elderly men (suspected of proneness to indecent exposure).

dirty week-end Week-end of sexual activity away from home.

dirty work at the cross-roads Unspecified misdoing.

disc-jockey See DJ.

dischuffed Displeased.

disco Entertainment, or place of entertainment, where recorded popular music is played.

dish
1. [n.] Attractive woman or man.
2. [v.] Spoil. Ruin. Defeat.
   - *Dish one's chances.*

dish it out Punish. Scold.

dish out Distribute. Inflict.

dishy Attractive. (Of person.)

distance, the full
1. The allotted time.
2. **go the (full) distance** Last for the allotted time (usu. in a sporting event).

ditch [v.]
1. Abandon. Cast away. Leave in the lurch.
2. (Of pilot or aircraft) Make forced landing in sea.

dither, all of a In a state of nervous anticipation or excitement.

dithers Feelings of anxiety.

dive
1. Cheap place of entertainment.
2. (In sport) Pretended fall or injury. Usu. **take a dive**.

divvy Dividend.

do
1. [v.] Cheat. Rob.
2. [n.] Social event. Entertainment.
3. [v.] (Used very loosely in a variety of contexts.) Place at a disadvantage. Punish. Defeat. Attack. Ruin. Kill. Reprimand. Arrest.
   - *I got done for speeding.*

4. [v.] Have sexual intercourse with.
5. [v.] Visit (as tourist).
6. [v.] Satisfy.
   - *That will do me.*

do a Act like.

do a bunk Vanish. Depart hastily.

do a job Commit a crime.

do down Get the advantage of. Criticise. Cheat.

do for
1. Ruin. Destroy. Defeat.
2. Undertake domestic work for.
3. Enhance.
   - *It does nothing for . . .* It does not enhance . . .

do-gooder Person engaged in social work.

do in Kill. Defeat.

do one's bit Play a part in a cause or undertaking.

do one's nut Be very angry or worried.

do one's stuff Do what one has promised, or what is expected of one.

do one's (own) thing Do as one wishes. Do something one is good at.

do oneself proud *or* **well** Live very comfortably.

do over Assault.

do proud Behave generously or hospitably towards.

do something (standing) on one's head Do something easily. Also **with one('s) hand (tied) behind one's back, with one's eyes closed**.

do the dirty on Treat badly (usu. by betraying expectations).

do the handsome (thing) Behave well or generously (towards someone).

do the trick Achieve the object.

do time Serve a prison sentence.

do to death Overdo.

do with, I could I should like.

do without, I could I do not like.

doc Doctor.

dock, in Being repaired or serviced. In hospital.

doctor [v.] Render sterile. (Of animals.)

doctor ordered, what the What is necessary.

doddle Very simple undertaking.

dodge Clever expedient.

dodge the column Evade one's obligations.

dodgy Uncertain. Risky.

dog Fellow. Also see **lame dog**.

dog bites dog Like criticises like. Also opp. **dog doesn't eat dog**.

dog-collar Clergyman's stiff collar.

dog-end Cigarette end.

dog-fight Indiscriminate and unorganised fight.

dog-house, in the In disgrace.

dog's back leg, straight as (*or* like) a Crooked.

dog's breakfast Mess.

dog's dinner Meal of scraps of left-over food. Used met. for (sometimes unsuccessful) attempt at stylish dress. Hence **done up like a dog's dinner** Wearing conspicuous (or incongruous) clothes.

dogs, go to the
1. Decline in standards, success, esteem, etc. Become dissipated.
2. **the dogs** Greyhound races.

doggo Inconspicuous (usu. temporarily). Usu. **lie doggo**.

dogsbody Person who does menial tasks.

doings Anything of which the speaker cannot remember the name.

dole, (on) the (In receipt of) State payment during un-
employment.

doll Young woman (usu. attractive and smartly dressed).

doll up Dress smartly and stylishly.

dollop Small soft lump (e.g. dough, putty). Portion of any similar substance.

dolly(-bird) Attractive girl. Girl-friend.

done! Agreed!

done for Exhausted. Worn out. Incapable of further use or
effort.

done in Tired out.

done thing, the What is normally or socially acceptable. See **not
done**.

done up Assaulted. Beaten.

donkey's years (For) a long time.

don't mind me Have no concern for me. (Usu. sarcastic excl.)

doodah An object of which the name has been forgotten by the
speaker.

doofer Same as **doodah**.

doolally Mad. Usu. **go (all) doolally** Behave eccentrically.

doorstep Very thick sandwich.

dope
1. Narcotic (usu. hashish, heroin or cannabis).
2. Full information on a particular subject.
3. Fool.
4. [v.] Administer drugs to.
5. **doped** Under influence of drugs.
6. **dope fiend** Drug addict.

dop(e)y
1. Half asleep.
2. Slow. Dull-witted.

dorm Dormitory.

dose Venereal infection.

dose of salts, like a Very quickly.

doss [n.] Temporary bed.

doss (down) [v.] Sleep, often in makeshift circumstances.

doss-house Lodging house (usu. very cheap).

doss out Sleep in the open.

dosser One who sleeps in a variety of places. Tramp. Vagrant.

dot (a person one) Strike (a person) (usu. in the face).

dotted line, sign on the Sign one's name as agreement.

dotty Crazy.

double-cross Betray. Fail to do what one has promised. (Usu. criminal slang).

double shuffle Rearrangement. Deception.

double-take Delayed reaction (usu. exaggerated facial expression), by person experiencing surprise at something which does not strike him immediately. (Often theat. trick.)

dough Money.

down
1. [adj.] Depressed.
2. [v.] Drink, usu. quickly.

down in the dumps Depressed. Miserable.

down on, have a Be severe on or prejudiced against.

down the drain *or* **pan** Lost. Spent. Wasted. Mis-spent. Squandered. Finished. Ruined.

down the hatch! (Toast.)

down to the ground Completely.

down tools
1. End work.
2. Go on strike.

down-town [adj.] At or near the centre of large towns and cities. Characteristic of urban squalor.

downer Depressant drug.

dozy Same as **dopey**.

drag [n.]
1. Bore. Unrewarding effort.
2. Female clothing worn by men. Usu. **in drag** Wearing such clothing.
3. Puff of a cigarette.
4. **drag-racing** Type of car-racing.

dragged up Educated. Reared. [Derog.]

draggy Boring.

drain-pipes Trousers with narrow legs.

drapes Curtains [usu. theat.].

drat (it) Mild excl.

draw a blank Have no result or luck.

draw it mild Refrain from exaggeration.

draw the line Set a limit to what one is willing to do, say, concede, etc.

dream, like a Exactly as one would wish.

dream up Invent.

dressed to death or **(fit) to kill** or **up to the nines** or **up like a dog's dinner** Very smartly dressed.

dribs and drabs Small and irregular quantities.

drill
1. Right way of doing something. Arrangements.
2. **what's the drill?** How do we do this?

drink [n.] Sea.

drink like a fish Drink (alcohol) excessively.

drip Stupid, feeble or uninteresting person.

drive up the wall Irritate intensely.

droop, brewer's Loss of sexual appetite in men, supposed to be result of too much drinking.

drop a bomb Create a shock.

drop a brick Behave tactlessly. Make an error.

drop acid Take LSD.

drop dead! Excl. of disbelief, refusal or contempt (usu. hostile or abusive, but not always).

drop, fit *or* **ready to** Worn out.

drop (someone) in it Cause (someone) inconvenience, trouble, etc., by one's own action.

drop in on Visit casually.

drop it Cease.

drop like a hot potato Abandon quickly.

drop on Have a piece of luck.

dropped on (from a dizzy height) Severely reprimanded.

drop out
1. [v.] Adopt an unconventional way of life. Refuse to accept the normal conventions of society.

drop-out [n.] Person who does this.

dropsy Tendency to drop things. [Facet.]

drum, tight as a Very drunk.

drum up Obtain. Make (e.g. tea).

drunk [n.] Intoxicated person.

dry up
1. Forget one's lines while acting a part on the stage. (Usu. **dry**.)
2. Become silent.

duchess Wife. Mother. Woman.

duck
1. Evade (usu. a problem or responsibility).
2. Term of endearment. Also **ducky, ducks**.

ducky Fetching.

dud
1. [adj.] False. Incompetent. Failing to operate. Useless. Worthless.
2. [n.] Useless imitation.
3. [n.] Incompetent person.

duds Clothes.

dude Dandy.

dude ranch Farm or ranch operated by persons from city who imitate countryman's style of dress, etc.

duff
1. Inaccurate. Inferior. Worthless. Useless.
2. **duff (up)** Punch. Beat.

duffer Incompetent person. Simpleton. Bungler.

dukes Fists.

dumb Stupid. Also **dumb-head** Foolish person.

dumb waiter Elevator. [RS]

dumdum Foolish person.

dump
1. [n.] Unattractive, dull, boring place.
2. [v.] Place. Set down. Abandon.

dumps, down in the Depressed.

dunno I don't know.

dust one's jacket Thrash one.

dust-up Quarrel. Row.

dustman Sleep (personified). [Juv.]

dusty, not so Fairly good.

Dutch Wife. (Usu. **old Dutch**.)

Dutch comfort Negative consolation.

Dutchman, I'm a Emph. expression of disbelief used with sentences beginning 'If . . .'
• *If that's art, I'm a Dutchman.* That is not art.

dying duck in a thunderstorm, like a Looking absurdly forlorn or bedraggled.

dynamite
1. Highly efficient person.
2. Dangerous situation. Tense or emotional situation likely to suddenly explode.
3. Heroin.

E

eager beaver See **beaver**.

ear-bashing Reprimand.

ear, by Without preparation. Usu. **play by ear** Do as seems appropriate when the time comes, the occasion arises, etc., without preparation.

earful Reprimand. Complaint.

ear-hole, on the Engaged in swindling.

ears flapping, with Avid for information.

ears, up to one's Very busy. Very involved.

ears were flapping, my etc. I (etc.) was listening with great interest (usu. to gossip).

earth, on Added to numerous interrogatives (why, what, how, who, etc.) to give emph., sense of surprise, exasperation, etc.
  • *Where on earth can it be?*

earth, the A large sum of money.
  • *It cost me the earth.*

earthly
  1. [adj.] Whatsoever.
    • *No earthly use.* No use whatsoever.
  2. [n.] Chance.
  3. **(stand) not an earthly (chance)** (Have) no chance whatsoever.

ear-wigging Reprimand.

easy
1. Indifferent.
   - *I'm easy.*
2. **easy meat** Easy to obtain, do, etc.
3. **easy on the eye** Good-looking.
4. **easy as pinching money from a blind man, as shelling peas** *or* **as winking** Very easy.
5. **easy does it** Don't hurry. Remain calm.

easy street, in In wealthy or comfortable circumstances.

eat Annoy.
   - *What's eating him?*

eat one's head off Eat heartily.

eat the hind (back) legs off a donkey, could Be very hungry.

eating irons Cutlery.

eats Food.

edge on, have the Be slightly better than.

eff Evasion of **fuck*** Usu. **eff off, effing.**

eff and blind Use coarse language.

effort Attempt. Piece of work.

egg Person.

egg-box
1. Large block of flats or offices, etc., having numerous identical compartments.
2. [adj.] Constructed thus.

egg-head Person interested in intellectual matters.

egg on one's face, get Be embarrassed by the consequences of one's own action.

ego-trip Period of indulgence in egocentric behaviour.

Egyptian PT Sleep.

eight See **one over the eight**.

elbow, (get *or* **give) the** (Receive or give) dismissal or rebuff.

elbow grease Vigorous rubbing, or any form of manual effort.

emperor's new clothes Something which does not exist (despite 'the emperor's' conviction to the contrary).

empire-builder
1. One who assumes or creates additional responsibilities to increase his own power (or chance of promotion).
2. **empire** Responsibilities of this kind. Any responsibilities or sphere of influence.

end
1. See **get one's end away** and **have one's end away**.
2. **no end** Very much.
3. **no end** A great amount or number of.
4. **go (in) off the deep end** Become very annoyed.
5. **the end** The limit of what can be tolerated.

enemy, the Time.
- *How goes the enemy?* What's the time?

engineer [v.] Plot. Manoeuvre.

enough to make a cat laugh Very amusing.

erk
1. Low-grade workman.
2. Beginner.
3. Gen. term of abuse.

evaporate Disappear suddenly.

even Stephen Fair shares. Evenly balanced.

ever so Extremely.

every bit as Quite as.

every man jack Everybody.

everything but the kitchen sink A large quantity of miscellaneous objects.

everything in the garden is lovely Everything is satisfactory.

ex Former wife or husband.

excuse my French Pardon my bad language.

expecting Pregnant.

eye, all my Nonsense.

eyeball to eyeball Face to face, usu. aggressively.

eye in a sling, have one's Be defeated. Be in difficulty.

eyes stick out like organ-stops (*or* chapel hat-pegs), one's One expresses considerable amazement.

eyeful, an
1. Something or someone interesting or attractive to look at.
2. **have (take) an eyeful** Look with interest.

eyelashes, hang on by one's Succeed in persevering in difficult circumstances.

eyewash Bunkum. Something done or said to make a good impression, rather than in the interests of honesty, correctness or efficiency. Verbal camouflage. Misleading (often flattering) statement.

F

FA
1. Nothing.
2. **sweet FA** Nothing. [Emph.]

fab Extremely pleasing. Also **fabulous**.

face-ache
1. Miserable person.
2. Term of address. [Facet.]

face as long as a fiddle, have a Look gloomy, miserable.

face-fungus Beard. Moustache.

face like the back of a bus, etc., **have a** Be ugly.

face on, put one's Apply one's make-up.

fade
1. [n.] Failure. Disappointment.
2. **do a fade** Depart.

fade away Depart unobtrusively.

faff [v.] Waste time. Behave desultorily. Idle. Usu. **faff around**.

fag
1. Cigarette.
2. Boring or tiresome piece of work.
3. Abbr. of **faggot (1)**

fag-end
1. Cigarette end.
2. End.

fagged (out) Tired. Exhausted.

faggot
1. Male homosexual. (adj.) **faggy**.
2. Term of address to a naughty child.
3. Pieces of cooked mince-meat in rissole.

fail-safe [adj.] Providing a means of achieving safety in the event of mishap.
- *Fail-safe device, mechanism,* etc.

faintest, have not the Have no idea.

fair Thorough. Complete.

fair cop Justifiable arrest.

fair crack of the whip, a A fair deal.

fair do's
1. Let there be fairness in dealing.
2. Fair and equal shares.
3. Mild excl. Please be fair.

fair enough Agreed.

fair to middlin(g) Moderately well (in health, etc.).

fairy Homosexual male.

fall down on Make a mistake in.

fall for Be greatly attracted by.

fall-guy
1. Scapegoat.
2. Victim.

fall over oneself Be very eager.

falling off a log, as easy as Very easy.

family way, in the Pregnant.

famous last words Facet. or ironic response to a statement, to express incredulity.

fancy! just fancy! fancy that! Excl. of surprise.

fancy man
1. Lover.
2. Pimp.

fancy oneself Have unduly high opinion of oneself.

fancy pants Over dressed, conceited person (usu. male).

fancy piece *or* **woman** Mistress.

fanny
1. Same as **backside**.
2. Female private parts.
3. **Fanny Adams** Same as **FA** [Abbr.]

fantastic Extraordinarily pleasing.

far back Affected (usu. in speech).

far out Advanced. Progressive. Very interesting or captivating. Idiosyncratic. Outside one's normal experience. [Pop.]

fart*
1. Person disapproved of. Also **fart-arse**.
2. Thing of small value. (E.g.
   - *Not worth a fart.*)
3. **fart about** *or* **around** Waste time. Also **fart-arse about** *or* **around**.

fast one, pull a Gain advantage by unfair action.

fast-talk [v.] Persuade.

fat
1. Pleasing. [Pop.]
2. Wealthy.

fat cat Rich person.

fat chance, a Not much chance.

fat lot, a Very little.

father and mother of a (row, etc.), the A severe, tremendous, terrific (row, etc.).

favour [v.] Resemble.

fearful Annoying. Considerable.

fearfully Very.

fed up
1. Bored. Depressed. Disgruntled. Having had too much.
2. **fed (up) to the back teeth** Emph. form of the above.

feed
1. Performer who supplies comedian with cues for jokes.
2. **feed one's face** Eat (but usu. used in a critical sense).
3. **feed the brute** Feed one's husband. (Common advice to newly-wed girls.)

feel free Help yourself.

feel rough Feel unwell. See **death (warmed-up).**

feel the draught Suffer inconvenience and hardship (usu. financial).

feel up Fondle sexually.

feisty Exuberant.

festering Emph. adv. & adj. expressing distaste, annoyance, etc.

fetch (a person) one Strike (him) a sharp blow.

fettle [v.] Repair. Solve. Put right.

few, have a Have a few drinks.

fiddle
1. [n.] & [v.] Cheat. Swindle. Also **be on the fiddle** Be involved in swindling.
2. A detailed piece of work (usu. causing irritation). [Adj.] **fiddly.**
3. **fiddle (with)** Fidget. Also [n.] **fiddler.**
4. **fiddle about** Behave restlessly or to no purpose.

fiddle-faddle [v.] Waste time.

fiddle-sticks! Mild excl. of disagreement.

field-day, have a Enjoy success.

field, play the Try all available options.

fight with the gloves on Fight viciously.

fighting drunk Drunk and consequently quarrelsome.

fighting talk *or* **words** A challenge. Provocation. Defiant response.

figure [v.] Make sense. Be likely.

figure out Understand. Consider with a view to reaching conclusion.

fill in
1. Thrash. (Usu. facet. threat.)
2. Inform. Bring (someone) up to date.
   - *I filled him in.*

filly Attractive young woman.

finagle [v.] Behave dishonestly.

finangle See **finagle**.

fine and dandy Excellent.

fine old time, a A very enjoyable time.

fine weather for ducks Very wet weather.

finger
1. Rough measure of drink.
2. [v.] Name person responsible (usu. offender).

finger on, put the Inform against.

finger out, get (pull *or* **take) one's** Work harder or faster. Begin to work. Move more quickly. Buckle to.

fingers are all thumbs, one's One is clumsy with one's hands.

fink
1. Objectionable person.
2. Informer. Same as **grass (2)**.

fire [v.] Dismiss (person from employment).

fire away Begin.

fire-bug Pyromaniac.

fire-eater Hot-tempered person.

fire-water Strong alcoholic drink (usu. of cheap and poor quality).

fireproof Safe from blame or danger. Invulnerable.

fireworks Trouble.

firm up Make firm (arrangements etc.).

first-nighter One who habitually attends first performances of plays in West End.

first thing Early in the day. Before anything else.

fish
1. Person. Usu. **odd, queer fish** Rather strange person.
2. **Fish out** Search for and find.

fish-face Term of abuse.

fish to fry, have other Have other responsibilities, possibilities.

fishy
1. Arousing suspicion.
2. **fishy about the gills** Pale. Depressed.

fist at *or* **of, make a (good, bad)** Make an attempt (well, successfully; badly, unsuccessfully) at.

fit, throw (have) a React with sharp, outspoken, shocked surprise. [Emph.]

fit to bust, laugh Laugh exceedingly.

fit to drop Exhausted.

fit to kill Excessively. Strikingly.

fit to turn a dog out, not Very inclement weather.

fix
1. Be revenged on.
2. Adjust, conclude, arrange, etc. Also **fix up**.
3. **to be fixed up** To have made arrangements satisfactorily.
4. **fix one's face** Adjust one's make-up (of women).
5. [n.] Dose (usu. injection of drugs)
6. [v.] Take drugs (usu. by injection).

fixer Agent (usu. musical).

fizz
1. Champagne. Any effervescent drink.
2. **fizz (along)** Move quickly.
3. **full of fizz** Excited. Elated. Very active.

fizzer
1. Person or thing much admired.
2. **on a fizzer** In trouble. Subject to a disciplinary process.

fizzing
1. Excellent.
2. Excitingly quick.

flack See **flak**.

flag-wagging [adj.] Patriotic. Jingoistic. Also [n.].

flak Criticism. Blame. Reproof.

flake out
1. Fall asleep because of extreme exhaustion.
2. Faint.

flaked out Exhausted.

flame Sweetheart. (Usu. **old flame** Former sweetheart.)

flaming Emph. adj. & adv. expressing annoyance.

flanker, do (work) a Out-manoeuvre, outwit by indirect tactics.

flannel Mere talk (usu. intended to deceive, or conceal e.g. the speaker's ignorance). Nonsense. Boastfulness. Flattery. Also [v.].

flannel through Talk one's way out of (difficulty, etc.).

flanneller One who talks **flannel**.

flap
1. [n.] State of excitement, confusion or anxiety.
2. [v.] Become agitated.

flapper Young girl of gay 1920s society.

flash [v.]
1. Show off ostentatiously.
   • *Flash one's money around.* Spend showily.
2. Commit indecent exposure. Hence **flasher** Male sexual exhibitionist.

flat
1. [n.] Puncture.
2. [adj.] Completely.
   • *Flat broke* Penniless.

flat-footed Clumsy. Tactless.

flat-head Idiot.

flat spin State of agitation.

flea-bag
1. Sleeping-bag.
2. Term of abuse. (Not in polite use.)

flea-bite Trivial sum, object, matter. Usu. **mere flea-bite** A matter of no consequence.

flea-pit Low-class lodging, cinema, etc.

flicks Cinema.

flier See **flyer**.

flies on him, there are no He is very alert and efficient.

flimsies Insubstantial, small or translucent garments (usu. female and intended to be sexually provocative).

fling [n.] Spree.

flip
1. Brief trip (usu. by plane).
2. [v.] Become excited to the point of ecstasy. [Pop.] Also **flip one's top** *or* **lid** Lose one's self-control.
3. [adj.] Casual, flippant.

flip side The other side of a gramophone record.

flipping Mildly emph. adj. & adv. of no meaning.

float
1. [n.] Loan.
2. [v.] Move in leisurely manner.

floater Blunder.

flog
1. Steal.
2. Sell.
3. Defeat.
4. Move by painful effort.
   - *Don't flog yourself.* Don't overdo things.

floor [v.]
1. Knock down.
2. Baffle. Perplex.

floozie Young woman (usu. rather blowzy). Girl-friend.

flop
1. [n.] Failure.
2. [v.] Fail.

flop-house Cheap lodging-house.

flower power Hippies' philosophy adhering to love, brotherhood, etc., as powerful forces. [Pop.] Also **flower people** People (usu. young) adhering to this philosophy.

91

flu Influenza.

fluff
1. See **little bit of fluff**.
2. [v.] Bungle. Make a mistake.
3. [n.] Mistake, often in reciting lines, playing music or game, etc.

flummox Bewilder.

flunder Enter boisterously. Fall noisily.

flunk Fail (exam).

flush [adj.] Having plenty of money.

flush out Discover in hiding, eject and capture.

flutter [v.] Gamble in small way. Also [n.].

fly Artful. Knowing. Alert.

fly-by-night
1. Unreliable person.
2. Debtor who evades creditors.

fly off the handle Suddenly lose one's temper or take offence.

fly pitch Stall or other selling-place used by street traders.

flyer
1. Lively and pretty girl.
2. Any thing or body capable of unusual speed.
3. Ambitious or successful person. Also **high-flyer**.
4. **flyer, take (come) a** Fall down heavily.

foggiest (notion), not have the Have no idea whatever.

fold(-up) Cease (usu. of business).

folks Parents.

fool to oneself, be a Act contrary to one's own interests (usu. deliberately, e.g. out of kindness).

foot See **my foot!**

foot it Walk.

foot-rot Disease of the foot (e.g. Athletes' foot).

foot-slogger Pedestrian. Infantry soldier.

footer The game of football.

footle
1. Waste time on trivialities.
2. [n.] **footler** One who does this.
3. [adj.] **footling** Foolishly trivial.

footsie *or* **footsy, play** Rub one's foot against someone else's (usu. secretly, e.g. under a table) sensually.

footy Same as **footer** and **footsie**.

for crying out loud! Excl. of displeasure, disagreement, protest, etc.

for free Without charge.

for good and all Permanently.

for it Due for punishment.

for keeps Permanently.

for nuts Same as for **toffee**.

for Pete's sake Emph. addition to sentence, expressing (mild) annoyance.

for real Serious. Not to be taken lightly. Genuine.

for the hell of it For amusement only.

for the high jump Likely to be reprimanded or punished.

for the life of me Emph. addition to a negative.

for the love of Mike Same as **for Pete's sake**.

for toffee To any degree whatever.
- *I can't sing for toffee.*

force, the The Police Force. A policeman.

fork out *or* **up** Hand over. Pay.

form Previous record, usu. criminal.

forty fits, have Be very alarmed. [Emph.]

forrader More forward.

foul [adj.] Revolting.

foul up [v.] Disorganise (plans, etc.).

foul-up [n.] Muddle.

four eyes
1. Person wearing spectacles.
2. [adj.] **four-eyed** Wearing spectacles. Also occ. term of abuse.

fourpenny one [n.] Blow.

fourth estate, the The press.

frame
1. Invent and bring evidence to support a false complaint or to bring about a faked result. Also [v.] **frame up**.
2. [n.] **frame-up** The act of doing this. Conspiracy.
3. **be framed** Be the victim of such a conspiracy, betrayal or trick.

frat Fraternise.

fraught
1. Risky. Causing anxiety.
2. Very busy.

freak Enthusiast.

freak out [v.] Indulge in unconventional, wild or irrational behaviour (often associated with drugs, popular music, etc.). [Pop.]

freak-out
1. [n.] Event where extraordinary behaviour (see **freak out**) occurs. Also facet. for any very staid event.
2. [n.] Person who **freaks out**.

free country, it's a What is proposed is legal.

freebie Free gift.

freeze out Exclude.

French, excuse my Forgive my bad language.

French letter Male contraceptive sheath. Also **Frenchy**.

fresh
1. Impertinent.
2. Over-intimate.

fresh-air fiend Person with strong belief in the therapeutic effects of fresh air (usu. by taking exercise).

freshen up Wash or revive oneself. Restore to original freshness.

fresher Undergraduate in first year at university.

fret one's gizzard *or* **guts** Worry.

frig*
1. Copulate.
2. Masturbate.

frig about Waste time. Behave ineffectually.

frig off!* Go away.

frigging Emph. adj. expressing annoyance.

frighteners on, put the Exert pressure on (person) by causing fear.

frightful Very great. Extreme.

frightfully Extremely.

frillies Feminine underwear.

fringe
1. [adj.] Peripheral, unofficial, not well established, minor. (Often theat., of experimental performances.)
2. [n.] Activities of this kind (usu. theat.).

frisk Search a person (usu. for hidden evidence, weapons, etc.).

Frog, Froggie (*or***-y)** Frenchman. [Derog.] Also [adj.].

frog in the throat, have a Experience hoarseness.

front [v.] Act as **front man**.

front man Member of criminal gang who looks and sounds respectable and whose function is to draw attention away from the activities of his associates.

front runner Thing or person most likely to succeed in the circumstances.

frost Failure (usu. of an event).

frowsty Unwholesome. Stuffy.

frozen mitt, the Refusal. Rejection. Lack of welcome.

fruit, old Affectionate term of address.

fruity Strongly suggestive or over-vigorous (usu. of language).

fuck*

    1. [v.] Have sexual intercourse with.

    2. [n.] Sexual intercourse.

    3. Excl. of annoyance. Also in numerous expressions expressing irritation, etc.

    4. **fuck off** Go away.

    5. **fuck about** Waste time. Behave ineffectually. Potter. (Implies displeasure.)

    6. **fuck all** Nothing. See FA.

fucked* Exhausted. Also **fucked and far from home**.

fucker* Same as **bastard (2)**.

fucking* Emph. adj. & adv. expressing strong disapproval.

fuddy-duddy Fussy, old-fashioned, ineffectual (person).

fudge Make a mistake.

fudge up Invent a rather makeshift, unsatisfactory solution.

fug Thick, warm (usu. stuffy) atmosphere. [adj.] **fuggy**.

full blast, (at) Full speed. Fully operative.

full distance, go *or* **last the** Survive throughout the scheduled time.

full of beans In good health or spirits. Lively.

full steam ahead Proceed without delay at maximum speed.

full up Replete. Completely occupied.

fun and games Amusement. (Often ironical.)

funeral Responsibility.

    ● *It's his own funeral.* It's his own responsibility.

fungus Beard. Also **face fungus**.

funk

    1. [n.] Fear. Cowardice. Also **blue funk** Terror.

    2. [v.] Show cowardice (usu. by evasion, refusal to act, etc.). Try to avoid. Show fear.

funk-hole Refuge for coward.

funky
1. Cowardly.
2. Fashionable.
3. Characterised by strong feeling.

funny Slightly unwell.

funny business Trickery, or any doubtful or suspicious matter or activity.

funny farm Mental hospital.

funny-ha-ha Comical.

funny, make a Say something amusing.

funny-peculiar Perplexing. Curious.

fury, like Furiously.

fuse, have a short Be easily moved to anger or loss of control.

fuss-pot Fussy person. Also **fuss-budget**.

fut See **phut**.

future (in it), no No point (in it).

fuzz Police.

G

g and t Gin and tonic.

G-string Extremely small garment to cover private parts (usu. worn by night-club dancers, strip-tease performers, etc.).

gab
1. [n.] Chatter.
2. [v.] Talk too much. See **gift of the gab**.

gaff
1. Engagement, booking (of musician for concert. Ex. earlier meaning of 'cheap place of entertainment').
2. Home.
3. **blow the gaff** Reveal a secret.
4. **stand for the gaff** Endure the difficulties.

gaffer
1. Old man.
2. Boss (esp. publican, foreman).

gaga Senile. Foolish because of old age.

gal Girl.

gall Impudence.

gallivant Gad about. Move around rapidly.

game
1. Plan. Intention.
   - *What's his little game?*
2. **on the game** Involved in any (usu. dubious) undertaking, esp. prostitution.
3. See **give the game away**.

4. **game not worth the candle** Risk not worth taking. Worthless undertaking.

gammy Lame; wounded; disabled; sore; painful or incapacitated (usu. because of injury).

gamp Umbrella.

gander [n.] Look.

gang
1. Group (often used disapprovingly).
2. **gang-bang** Act of sexual intercourse between one female and several successive males. Also **gang-shag***.
3. [v.] **gang up (on)** Conspire (to oppose or damage).

gannet Greedy person.

gargle [n.] & [v.] Drink (beer, etc.).

garn! Go on! (Excl. of surprise or disbelief.)

gas
1. [n.] Vapid talk.
2. Petrol.
3. [v.] Talk idly.
4. **a gas** Fun. An amusing situation. Also **a gasser**.
5. **step on the gas** Go more quickly.
6. **gas and gaiters** Nonsense.

gasbag Person who talks too much.

gash Spare. Available.

gasket, blow a Erupt angrily.

gasper Cigarette.

gasping In urgent need (usu. **for a smoke** *or* **drink**) of a cigarette (or drink).

gathering of the clans Meeting together of relations or like-minded people.

gawd! God! (Excl.)

gawk *or* **gawp** Stare.

gay [adj.] and [n.] Homosexual. Also **gay as a row of pink tents** Very homosexual.

gayness Homosexuality.

gay old Very enjoyable.

gay old dog Lively elderly person.

gazump Verbally agree to sell (usu. a house) and then increase the price. **be gazumped** Fail to conclude house-purchase because the verbally agreed price was subsequently increased.

gear
1. [n.] Narcotics, usu. heroin.
2. Fashionable clothing.
3. **(the) gear** [adj.] Very pleasing. Genuine.

geared (up) Fitted. Prepared for. Ready.

gee (whiz)! Excl. of mild surprise.

gee(-gee) Horse.

gee up Hurry up.

geezer Man.

gel [v.] Take shape. Form a coherent pattern or whole. Also **jell**.

gelly Gelignite.

gelt Money.

gemini! Excl. of surprise.

gen Information. Knowledge. News.

gen up on
1. Learn. Study.
2. **gen oneself up** Inform oneself.
3. **(all) genned-up** Well informed.

gent Gentleman (usu. facet.).

gents Public lavatory for men.

gentleman of fortune Criminal.

Geordie Northumbrian.

george Lavatory.

gertcher! Excl. of contempt or derision.

get
1. Outwit.
   • *This part of the problem gets me.*

2. Understand.
  * *I get you.*
3. Annoy.
4. [n.] Unpleasant person.
5. **get!** get off!

get a kick out of Enjoy.

get a load of Attend to. Look at.

get a move on
  1. Make an immediate start.
  2. Hurry.

get a word in edgeways Succeed in intervening in much talk.

get above oneself Become conceited.

get across
  1. Irritate. Annoy.
  2. Make understood.

get along with you! Mild excl. of friendly disbelief or reproof.

get at
  1. Mean.
    * *What is he getting at?* What does he mean?
  2. Influence (usu. in underhand way). Tamper with. Bribe.
  3. Find fault with.
    * *His boss is always getting at him.*
  4. Ridicule.

get away with
  1. Succeed (in any way, usu. unfairly, unexpectedly).
  2. Same as **get along with you**.

get busy Make a start (on a job).

get by Contrive. Manage satisfactorily.

get cracking Start.

get down Depress.
  * *The film got me down.*

get going
  1. Operate smoothly and vigorously.
  2. Start.

get home Make an impact.

get into Affect.
- *What's got into him?*

get it (in the neck) Be punished.

get it badly Be infatuated.

get it together Succeed.

get knotted! See **knotted**.

get lost! Dismissive excl.

get me? Do you understand me?

get off
1. **get off with** Achieve favour with one of the opp. sex.
2. Excl. Stop teasing! Also **get off it**.
3. **where one gets off** Where one's true position is. To stop disagreeable behaviour.
   - *I'll tell him where he gets off*. I'll stand no more of his nonsense.
4. **get off one's back** Stop applying pressure to one.

get off on the wrong foot Start badly.

get off one's chest Relieve one's feeling or mind by making a statement.

get on
1. Become old.
   - *He's getting on.*
2. **get on to** Reprimand. Communicate with.

get one's act together Succeed.

get one's end away *or* **in** Copulate.

get one's eye in Familiarise oneself.

get one's feet *or* **foot in** (*or* **under the table**) Establish oneself.

get one's goat Annoy one.

get one's hand in Familiarise oneself.

get one's head down Lie down to sleep.

get one's mad up *or* **out** Become angry.

get one's monkey up Arouse one's anger.

get one's own back (on) Be revenged (on).

get one's rag out Become angry.

get out!
   1. Go at once.
   2. Mild excl. of disbelief or surprise.

get-out [n.] Excuse. Escape. Evasion.

get outside of Eat.

get over Project. Inform. Make to understand.

get shot (shut) of Be rid of.

get some service in Acquire some experience.

get straight
   1. Arrange in order.
   2. Understand clearly.
      • *Get this straight!*

get stuck into
   1. Start.
   2. Work vigorously.

get stuffed Same as **get knotted** (under **knotted**).

get the bird
   1. Be rebuked.
   2. Be greeted with disapproval.

get the boot *or* **bullet** Be dismissed.

get the hang of Understand.

get the message See **message**.

get the needle Be annoyed or nervous.

get there Succeed.

get through to
   1. Communicate with (often by telephone).
   2. Make oneself understand.

get-together [n.] Meeting.

get-up [n.] Dress.

get up and go Ambition. Initiative.

get weaving Start.

get what's coming (to one) Receive (one's) just deserts.

get wise to Discover. Realise.

getaway
1. [n.] Escape.
2. [adj.] Used for escaping.
   • *Getaway car.*

getting at Trying to say or do.

ghastly Emph. adj. registering displeasure.

giddy
1. Emph. adj. (e.g. **the giddy limit** The most extreme limit one can tolerate).
2. **giddy goat** Irresponsible fool.
3. **play the giddy goat** Act irresponsibly or foolishly.

gift of the gab Power of fluent and effective speech.

gig Engagement, booking (usu. of musician for performance).

giggle A mildly amusing event or person. Also **a bit of a giggle**.

gimme Give (it) to me.

gimmick
1. Any device to catch the attention.
2. [adj.] **gimmicky** Superficially eye-catching. Impermanent. Insubstantial. [n.] **Gimmickry.**

gin and Jag(uar) Adj. phrase applied to people, districts, etc. of (newly) rich upper-middle class.

gin and it Gin with Italian vermouth.

gin palace Place of vulgarly ostentatious architecture, interior decoration, style, etc.

gin sling American drink.

ginger pop Ginger beer.

gip
1. [v.] Steal.
2. [n.] Pain. Punishment. Also **gippo**.

gippy tummy Upset stomach. Also **gyppy**.

Girl Friday Female secretary and/or personal assistant in offices, etc.

girlie
1. Term of address to young woman.
2. [adj.] Preoccupied with young women. e.g. **girlie-show** Entertainment in which dancing girls appear; **girlie-mag(azine)** Magazine devoted to pictures of nude or provocatively posed women.

git
1. Go away. (Excl.)
2. Person usu. one disapproved of. (Vulgar.)

give a (big) hand Applaud (generously).

give a tinkle [v.] Telephone.

give-away [n.] Revelation (e.g. of secret).

give (all) hell to Reprimand, punish severely (and numerous other expressions related to pain, e.g.
● *The lunch we had today is giving me hell*).

give it a rest Stop.

give it (to) Blame. Punish. Scold.

give one a talking to Rebuke.

give one best Admit defeat by one.

give over! Be silent.

give the glad hand Welcome.

give the go-over Desert. Disregard. Ignore. Refuse to recognise. Avoid.

give the show away Betray something, or allow it to be detected, accidentally or otherwise.

give what for Rebuke. Punish.

gizzard
1. Stomach.
2. **fret one's gizzard** Worry.
3. **stick in one's gizzard** Annoy one.

glad eye Inviting glance (usu. by lady).

glad-handing Welcoming effusively (usu. of public figure shaking hands with everyone). See **give the glad hand**.

105

glad rags Smart clothing.

glam
1. [n.] Glamour.
2. [v.] Glamorous.

glam oneself up [v.] Take considerable care with one's appearance. Also **get yourself glammed up**.

glamour girl *or* **pants** *or* **puss** Attractive girl.

glasshouse Military prison.

glimmer(ing), not a None.
- *Not a glimmer of sense.* No sense.

glitter [n.] Cosmetic, consisting of tiny pieces of reflective material stuck or sprayed (on hair, round eyes, etc.) to catch the light.

glitzy Glittering. Showy.

glorified Slightly improved.

glory, go to Die.

glory hole Cupboard or small room (usu. untidy).

glossy
1. [n.] Expensive magazine.
2. **the glossies** The expensive magazines.

gnat's pee *or* **piss** Beer of poor quality.

gnat's piss *or* **piss, like** Unpleasant to the taste.

go [n.]
1. Fashion.
   - *These shirts are all the go.*
2. Attempt.
   - *Have a go.* Make an attempt.
3. Success.
   - *Make a go of it.*
4. Chance. Opportunity.
   - *It's your go now.*
5. See **no go, on the go, word go**.

go all out Concentrate every effort.

go aloft Die.

go and boil yourself *or* **your head** Dismissive excl. (usu. impatient or contemptuous).

go and eat coke Same as **go and boil yourself**.

go at, have a Criticise.

go bald-headed for Attack. Undertake vigorously.

go-by See **give the go-by**.

go cold (on) Lose enthusiasm (for). Lose interest.

go down
1. Make an impact.
   • *The event went down very well.* The event succeeded.
2. Finish (of theat. performances only).
3. **go down like a lead balloon** Be unpopular. Be received with disapproval.
4. Go to prison.

go easy on someone Treat someone gently.

go easy with Use sparingly.

go for
1. Enjoy.
2. Attack. Blame.
3. Be acceptable to.
   • *That goes for all of us.*
4. **go for a burton** See **burton**.

go-getter Thrustingly ambitious person.

go-go dancer Night-club or cabaret dancer.

go hang
1. Be disregarded.
2. Go to hell (i.e. dismissive term of mild abuse).

go, have a Make an attempt.

go haywire See **haywire**.

go home Wear out; reach the end of the usefulness.
   • *I think the car's going home.*

go it
1. Be daring or extravagant.
2. Excl. of encouragement to act with determination.

107

go much on See **go on (1).**

go nap Wager everything.

go of, make a Succeed in.

go off
1. Give birth.
   - *When's your wife due to go off?*
2. **go off the deep end** Lose one's temper.

go on
1. Enjoy.
   - *I don't go much on rugby.* I don't enjoy rugby very much.
2. Talk a lot, usu. scoldingly.
3. Excl. of surprise, encouragement or disbelief.

go on about Complain about. Talk at tiresome length of.

go, on the Moving about. Busy.

go one better than Surpass.

go out Fall out of favour, fashion, use, etc.

go over big Achieve great success.

go over to Change to.

go over the top Behave or talk in an unacceptably extravagant, exaggerated or embarrassing way.

go phut Collapse. Break. Become useless.

go places Travel.

go slow Work deliberately slowly. (Form of industrial action.)

go-slow [n.] The act of doing the above.

go slow with Be sparing with.

go spare Become angry.

go steady with Be a constant companion of (a particular member of the opp. sex).

go the rounds Circulate.

go the whole hog Act with complete thoroughness.

go through
1. **go through the hoop** Endure an unpleasant experience.

2. **go through the motions** Pretend.
3. **go through with** Endure and complete.

go to blazes, hell, Jericho, Halifax *or* **the devil!** Excl. of contemptuous dismissal.

go to it Begin work.

go to pot Become useless.

go to the bad *or* **dogs** Deteriorate.

go to town Enjoy oneself. Celebrate. Do anything on an extravagant scale. Work or tackle energetically.

go up in the air Become very angry.

go west
1. Disappear.
2. Become useless.

goal See **own goal**.

goalie Goalkeeper.

goat, get one's Annoy one.

goat, play the Fool about.

gob
1. [n.] Mouth.
2. [v.] Spit.

gobstopper Large sticky sweet.

gobble [n.] Fellatio. Also [v.].

gobbler One who commits fellatio.

god-awful Very bad.

god-box Church.

God knows I don't know.

gods, the The gallery. (Theat.)

goer
1. One who tries hard (usu. of animals).
2. Lubricious person (usu. woman).

gofer Low-grade assistant who is paid to 'go for' this and that.

goggle-box Television set.

goggles Spectacles.

going-away dress Dress worn by bride leaving for honeymoon.

going for In favour of. Working out well for.

going spare Available (but see **spare**).

going strong Being vigorous, prosperous, successful.

going-over [n.] Strong criticism. Inspection. Thrashing.

goings-on Activities of any kind (often derog.).

gold-digger Person, usu. scheming woman, who cultivates the society of the rich in the hope of gain.

golden handshake Official present (usu. money) given to one who leaves employment (usu. to retire or because his services are no longer required).

golf widow Woman whose husband is often away playing golf.

gollop Devour greedily.

golly! Excl. of surprise.

gone Pregnant.

gone and done it Committed a rash or disastrous act.

gone on Infatuated with.

gonner Person dead or dying. One failing or failed. Useless or expended thing.

gong Medal.

goo Any sticky substance.

good as gold Extremely well behaved.

good egg! Excl. of satisfaction or approval.

good egg, a A good (helpful kind etc.) person.

good for *or* **on you (him, etc)!** Well done!

good gracious (me)! Excl. of surprise.

good hunting! Good luck in your enterprise!

good-looker Attractive person.

good luck to him I wish him well. (Often said with irony, or in disbelief of success.)

good money High wages.

good old Adj. expression of affection.

good on you! Well done!

good one, a An unlikely story, account, lie, explanation, etc.

good show! Well done! Splendid!

good sort Kind person.

good thing, on to a Concerned with something promising.

good value Worth having.

goods, the
1. Of excellent quality.
2. What is essential or required. Usu. **deliver the goods** Provide what is necessary.

goody
1. A good thing or person. (Jocular.) Hero. Opp. **baddy**.
2. Excl. of pleasure.

goody-goody
1. [adj.] Correct and virtuous in ostentatious way.
2. [n.] Person of this kind.
3. Excl. of pleasure.

gooey Sticky.

goof
1. [n.] Fool. [adj.] **goofy**.
2. [v.] Make a mistake.
3. [n.] Mistake.
4. **goofed** Drugged.

goo-goo eyes Large, round eyes.

gook Person of Chinese, etc., appearance. [Derog.]

goolies Testicles.

goon Idiot.

goop(y) Fool.

goose Poke in sensitive (usu. anal) region.

goosegog Gooseberry.

gorblimey Expr. of mild astonishment.

gormless Simple. Clumsy. Slow-witted.

got up to kill *or* **to the nines** Expensively or showily dressed.

governor, the
1. The chief, owner, manager, principal, head. Any superior or employer. (Occ. father.)
2. (without **the**) Term of deferential address to a stranger or superior.

grab Appeal to. Usu. **how does that grab you?** Does that (idea etc.) appeal to you.

grabs, up for Available for acquisition.

gradel(e)y Very well. Thorough. Complete.

graft
1. [n.] & [v.] Work. Often **hard graft**.
2. [n.] Underhand or criminal dealing. Also [v.].

grafter One engaged in **graft** (either sense).

grand, a A thousand (usu. pounds).

grand slam
1. Great success (usu. in several successive undertakings).
2. All-out attack or effort.

grape-vine Channels (or sources) of informal, secret or unofficial communication of information, rumour, etc. Usu. **on the grape-vine** Unofficially.

grass
1. Cannabis (marijuana).
2. One who informs the police, prison-warders, etc., of information for reward. Also [v.] To do this.
3. Betray.
4. **to be put out to grass** Retire (e.g. from employment). Be given a relatively inactive job.

grasser Same as **grass (2)**.

graveyard
1. [adj.] Gloomy.
2. **graveyard cough** Serious cough.

gravy Money.

gravy train Source of rapid personal profit.

gray mare Wife.

graze, put out to Same as **put out to grass**. See **grass (4)**.

grease
1. [n.] Flattery.
2. [v.] Ingratiate oneself.
3. **grease to** Ingratiate oneself with.
4. [v.] Cheat.
5. **grease the wheels** Enable an enterprise to run more smoothly.

grease-monkey Mechanic.

grease-spot [Lit.] A small amount of grease; hence, the state of a person as a result of heat, esp. hot weather.

greased lightning, like Very quickly indeed.

greaser
1. Sycophant. Disagreeable person.
2. Youth belonging to gang (usu., but not always, disruptive) of motorcycle-riders.

greasing Sycophancy.

great
1. Splendid. First-class.
2. **great on** An authority on.

great big Very big.

great guns See **blow great guns**.

great I am, the A conceited person.

great shakes See **shakes**.

great stuff
1. Anything excellent.
2. Excl. of pleasure.

great unwashed, the The working classes.

great wen, the London.

great white chief, the The boss. [Emph.]

greatest, the The most outstanding (person or thing).

greedy guts Glutton.

green as he's cabbage-looking, he's (etc.) **not so** He (etc.) is not as foolish as he seems.

green-back [n.] £1 note. Dollar bill.

green fingers, have Be successful at gardening.

green light Permission to proceed. Usu. **give** *or* **get the green light**.

gremlin Malicious devil supposedly responsible for accidents, malfunctioning, etc. (usu. in machinery).

griff Information. News.

grind
1. Usu. **daily grind** Hard monotonous work.
2. [n.] Sexual intercourse.
3. [v.] Have sexual intercourse. Also **do** *or* **have a grind**.
4. [v.] Masturbate.
5. **a grind** Drudgery. **hard grind** Very hard work.

grinding halt, come to a Stop (usu. suddenly or as a result of difficult circumstances). [Emph.]

gripe Complain. Also [n.].

grit
1. Determination. Staying-power.
2. [adj.] **gritty** Determined (usu. to succeed, in the face of difficulties).

grizzle Whimper, cry fretfully (usu. applied to children). Complain [n.] **grizzler, grizzle-guts**.

groove
1. [n.] Something excellent.
2. [v.] Give pleasure to. Enjoy oneself.

groove, in the In a state of high excitement. Performing well.

groovy Fashionable. Exciting. Excellent. Progressive. [Pop.]

grope Caress intimately. Also [n.].

grotty Very unattractive. Bad. Distasteful. Dirty.

grouch [n.] & [v.] Grumble.

ground floor
1. Lowest level (e.g. of a business, profession, etc.).
2. See **on the ground floor**.

groupie Girl living with several men. Member of a group.

grouse [n.] & [v.] Grumble.

grouser Complaining person.

grub Food.

grub-hunting Engaged in pursuits of a naturalist. **grub-hunter** Naturalist.

grumble-guts Complaining person.

grumps, the Fit of sulky behaviour.

gubbins Object of which one does not know (or has forgotten) the name, or which one is too busy or idle to name.

guessing Uncertain. Usu. **keep someone guessing** Keep someone in state of uncertainty.

guesstimate Estimate based on guesswork.

guff
1. Nonsense. Fatuous talk.
2. Bluff.
3. Information.

gum up Spoil, dislocate. Usu. **gum up the works** Cause confusion in matters; cause things to stop.

gum-tree, up a In a difficulty.

gumption Common sense.

gun, big Important person.

gunge Thick, greasy deposit or oily dirt.

gung-ho [adj.] Enthusiastically militaristic.

gunk Any thick, oily liquid.

gut Stomach.

guts
1. Courage. Staying power. [adj.] **gutsy**.
2. **hate one's guts** Dislike intensely.
3. **Sweat one's guts out** Work hard.
4. Basic essentials.
   • *The guts of the problem.*

gut-rot
1. Cheap strong drink.
2. Stomach pain or illness.

gutless Feeble; cowardly.

guts for garters, have one's Punish or reprimand one. (Usu. facet. threat.)

guv Same as **governor**. [Abbr.]

guy Fellow. Man.

guzunder Chamber pot.

gym Gymnasium. Physical training.

gyp Pain. **Give person (some) gyp** Scold him.

gypped Cheated.

H

hab-dabs, the (screaming) Extreme irritation.

hack [v.] Break into computer database without permission. **hacker** [n.] One who does this.

had Swindled.
- *You've been had.*

had it (in a big way), to have To be finished; to have failed. (Occ. to die.)

had one's day Passed the climax of usefulness or importance.

hair curl, make one's Make one very anxious, extremely apprehensive, frightened, worried on someone's behalf.
- *The risks mountaineers run are enough to make your hair curl.*

hair-do Woman's hair-styling.

hair down, let one's Enjoy oneself uninhibitedly.

hair, get in one's Irritate one.

hair on, keep one's Keep calm. Control one's temper.

hairs, have one by the short Have control over one. Have one at a disadvantage.

hairy Dangerous or dangerously exciting. Risky. Difficult. Unpleasant.

half
1. Half-pint.
2. **not half** Very much.
   - *He wasn't half mad.* He was very angry.

117

half a jiffy *or* **mo** *or* **tick** A brief space of time.

half-and-half
1. Mixture of equal portions of dissimilar things.
2. Mixture of ale and stout in equal portions.

half-baked
1. Silly.
2. Incompletely prepared or thought-out.
   • *A half-baked plan.*

half-cracked Slightly mad.

half-cut Fairly drunk.

half-inch [v.] Steal.

half round the bend Foolish.

half-seas over Drunk, or nearly.

half-slewed Half-drunk.

halfpenny worth (ha'p'orth) of tar, spoil the ship for a Achieve less than full satisfaction because of a slight economy.

halvers Halves. Usu. **go halvers** Share half-and-half.

ham
1. Theatrical performer or performance of exaggerated, ranting and generally outmoded style.
2. [v.] To behave like this. Also **ham it up**.
3. Enthusiast (usu. of amateur radio-broadcasting).
4. **hamming** Theatrical behaviour of exaggerated style.

ham-fisted Clumsy.

ham-handed Clumsy.

hammer [v.] Defeat soundly.

hammer (away) at Work hard (and continuously) at.

hammy In the manner of a **ham**.

hand, give a (big) Applaud (loudly).

hand it to Admire. Concede the skill or superiority of.

hand-me-downs
1. Ready-made clothing.
2. Used clothing.

handed (to one) on a plate Made easy (for one). Given freely (to one).

handful Strong-willed and difficult person to control (often child). Tricky task.

handle, fly off the Lose control of oneself.

handle (to one's name) Title. (Of person.)

handsome See **do the handsome.**

hang
1. [n.] Understand. Usu. **get the hang of** Comprehend.
2. **hang it!** Excl. of annoyance. (Also numerous expressions with **hang** to denote anger or disappointment.) Also **hang it all!**
3. **hang one on somebody** Hit somebody with the fist.

hang about! Wait a moment!

hang in there Await opportunity.

hang on Wait for a short time.

hang on by one's eye-lashes (-brows) Persevere in difficult circumstances. Be near to failure.

hang on to Retain.

hang out
1. [v.] Reveal.
   • *Let it all hang out.* Let all be revealed.
2. [v.] Live. Also [n.] **hang-out** Home.

hang out for Insist on (usu. acceptance of certain conditions).

hang-up
1. Preoccupation (usu. of personally troublesome or frustrating kind). Mental blockage. Complex or neurotic frustration. Difficulty. Grievance. [Pop.]
2. **hung up** Suffering from this.

hanged if, I'll be Emph. negative.
   • *Hanged if I will!* I won't under any circumstances!

hanger-on Worthless idler. (Social) parasite.

hangover Ill effects of heavy drinking.

hanky (*or* -ie) Handkerchief.

hanky-panky Trickery. Fraud. Underhand dealing.

ha'p'orth Halfpennyworth. **a ha'p'orth of difference** Very little or no difference.

happen (so) Perhaps.

happening Any impromptu or unusual event (usu. involving people in spontaneous activity) (e.g. theat.).

happy as Larry *or* **a sandboy** Very happy. Very carefree.

happy days *or* **landings!** Good luck! (Toast.)

happy event Birth of a baby.

hard
1. Hard labour in prison. [Abbr.]
2. **the hard stuff** Whisky, or any spirits.
3. [n.] Erection of penis. Usu. **have a hard on**.

hard at it Very busy.

hard-boiled (Of person) Inflexible. Unaccommodating. Stern.

hard case Incorrigible person (usu. lazy, dishonest or callous).

hard Cheddar Bad luck.

hard-faced Brazen. Shamelessly impudent.

hard-hat [adj.] Unyielding.

hard hit Deeply in love.

hard lines Unfortunate. Usu. **hard lines on** Unfortunate for.

hard luck story Tale of misfortune (usu. told to solicit help).

hard-nosed Uncompromising.

hard pushed Beset with difficulty. Hard pressed.

hard put to it In difficulty.

hard sell Direct and vigorous methods of salesmanship.

hard stuff Whisky, or any spirits.

hardy annual Topic, story, event which regularly occurs or comes up for discussion.

Harry
1. Meaningless and facet. component of numerous

expressions of which the two most common are **Harry flakers** Worn out (or **flaked out**) and **Harry starkers** Stark naked.
2. See **old Harry**.

has-been Person who has lost former proficiency.

hash
1. Hashish.
2. Muddle. Also **hash-up**.
3. **settle person's hash** Subdue person.
4. **hash up** Bungle.

hassle
1. [v.] Disagree, quarrel, make a fuss.
2. [n.] Controversy. Fuss. Bother. Nuisance. Quarrel.

hat See **talk through one's hat**.

hatch, match and dispatch Birth, marriage and death.

hatchet-man Unyielding person given to firm, forceful and uncompromising action.

hate one's guts Dislike one intensely.

haul over the coals Reprimand severely.

have
1. Defraud. Deceive. Trick.
  • *You've been had.*
2. Have sexual intercourse with.
3. **have had it** Be finished. Have failed. Be too late. (Occ. Die.) See also **it**.
4. **let one have it** Hit, punish or reprimand one.
5. [n.] Swindle.

have a go Make an attempt (occ. a rash one).

have a heart Be merciful.

have it away (together) Copulate.

have it in Copulate.

have it in for someone Be determined to punish or reprimand someone. Bear a grudge against someone.

have it made Be in a fortunate position.

have it off Copulate.

have it so good Enjoy advantages.

have kittens Be in a state of great excitement, anxiety or anger.

have one on
1. Deceive one.
2. Make fun of one.

have one's end away Copulate.

have the edge on See **edge**.

have the law on Take legal action against.

have what it takes Possess the necessary qualities.

hay, roll in the [n.] Sexual intercourse.

haywire
1. Confused. Hysterical. Mad.
2. **go haywire** Lose control.

he-man
1. Virile man.
2. [adj.] Very manly.

head
1. Headache. [Abbr.]
2. See **big head, soft in the head, knock on the head, off one's head, eat one's head off, head down**.
3. One who takes drugs, and who is also concerned with allied interests, e.g. meditation, pop, etc. (Suggests very serious involvement.)

head cook and bottlewasher One in authority. [Facet.] General factotum.

head, do something (standing) on one's Do something very easily.

head down, get one's Lie down to sleep.

head off, talk one's Talk incessantly.

head, off the top of one's Impromptu.

head-piece Brains.

head screwed on, have one's Be very sensible.

head-shrinker Psychologist; psychiatrist; psycho-analyst.

headache Problem. Responsibility.

header Headlong dive.

headlines, hit the Achieve prominence or publicity.

heads Lavatory.

heap Old car. Any old, worn-out machinery.

heap, knock *or* **strike all of a** Surprise violently.

heaps of Lots of.

hear myself think, I (etc.) **can't** Complaint about excessive noise.

hear of Eventually be blamed for.

hear tell that Hear it said that.

heart bleeds for, my I am not in the least sorry for (someone). (Always ironic in this way.)

heart, have a Please [Emph.]. Be merciful. Do not be so harsh.

heart in one's boots, have one's Be in a state of extreme depression or fear.

heart-throb Person, usu. man, of great physical attraction and glamorous personality (often film-star, etc.).

heart-to-heart, a [n.] Frank and intimate conversation. Also [adj.].

hearty [n.] Person rather ostentatiously devoted to practice of sporting activity.

heat Pressure.
  • *The heat is on.*

Heath Robinson [adj.] Grotesquely, deliberately and unnecessarily elaborate (usu. machinery).

heave Throw.

heave-ho, the (old) Dismissal. Snub.

heave up Vomit.

heavens! good heavens! Mild excl.

heavy
1. [n.] One who plays a serious, sombre or repressive role (Theat.). **come** *or* **do the heavy father** Give pompous and elaborate advice.
2. [adj.] Oppressive. Obscure. Bad. Deeply thoughtful. Involved. Extreme. Imponderable. Also [n.]. Person devoted to thoughts of this kind. [Pop.]
3. [n.] Violent thug. Strong bodyguard. Person employed to exercise physical force, usu. against people.

heavy petting See **petting**.

heck!
1. Mild excl. e.g.
   ● *Oh heck!*
2. Added to interrogative expressions for emph. e.g.
   ● *Who, what, why the heck does he . . . ?*
3. **what the heck?** What does it matter

hectic Wild, exciting, impassioned.

heebie-jeebies Intense depression or irritation.

heel Unpleasant person. See also **well-heeled**.

hefty [adv.] Very.

heist Robbery.

hell Used in numerous expressions as intensive, meaningless emph. e.g.
   ● *I wish to hell he'd stop.* I wish very much that he would stop.
   ● *It's a hell of distance.* It's a very long way.
1. Excl. Also **I'll go to hell, hell fire, hell's bells, hell's teeth**, etc.
2. **go to hell!** Go away! Also **get the hell out of here**.
3. **between hell and high water** In difficulties.
4. **come hell or (and) high water** Whatever the difficulties.
5. See **cat in hell's chance, snowball, give (all) hell to, all hell broke (was let) loose, play hell, like hell, raise hell, hope in hell, like hell, what the hell**.
6. **for the hell of it** Just for amusement.
7. **knock hell out of** Beat heavily.
8. **get hell** Be severely reprimanded.

hell-bent on Determined to.

hell broke(n) loose [n.] Chaos.

hell for leather At a reckless speed.

hell of a . . . , a A considerable.
- *A hell of a nuisance.*

helluva Same as **hell of a**.

helpless Drunk.

hen-party Party for women only.

hep
1. Well-informed, progressive.
2. **hep-cat** Devotee of jazz. Person who is **hep**.

herbert Fellow.

here goes Let us make a start.

here we go (again)!
1. Excl. complaining against repetitiousness.
2. Excl. signalling a beginning.

here's how *or* **mud in your eye** *or* **to us** Expression of good wishes. (Toast.)

herring pond, the The Atlantic Ocean.

het-up, (all) Heated with anger, anxiety or excitement.

hi! Common form of greeting.

hi-fi High fidelity gramophone and tape-recording equipment.

hide [n.] Skin.

hidey-hole Hiding place.

hiding [n.] Thrashing. Heavy defeat.

hiding to nothing, on a Doomed to failure.

high
1. [n.] Record.
   - *Prices have reached a new high.* Prices are higher than ever before.
2. [adj.] Drunk. Under the influence of drugs. Also **high as a kite**.
3. **the High** High Street (esp. Oxford).
4. [n.] Condition induced by taking drugs. Experience of exhilaration.

high and mighty Haughty. Arrogant.

high-brow [n.] Person with intellectual and culturally rarefied tastes. Also [adj.].

highball Whisky and ice served with water, soda water or ginger ale.

high camp [n.] Display (usu. artistic) of highly exaggerated nature. See **camp**.

high-hat
1. [adj.] Supercilious.
2. [v.] Behave arrogantly.

high jump, be for the Be about to be severely reprimanded or punished.

high old time Very enjoyable time.

high spot Outstanding feature. See **hit the high spots**.

high-stepper Fashionably and expensively dressed person.

high-up [n.] Person in authority. Also **higher-ups** Persons in authority.

high water See **hell (3) & (4)**.

hike [n.] & [v.]
1. Tour by walking.
2. Increase.

hiker One who walks long distances for pleasure.

hill-billy Yokel.

hill, over the See **over the hill**.

hind legs, get on one's Rise (to speak).

hip [adj.] Similar to **cool** and **with it** simultaneously.

hippy Young person of unorthodox life-style and beliefs, usually involving freedom from constraint, protest against conventionally organised society, reaction against normal moral standards, etc. Also [adj.]. See **drop out**.

hipster Same as **hep-cat**.

his nibs Any important individual. [Facet.]

hit
1. [v.] Arrive at.
2. [n.] Success.

hit-and-miss [adj.] Inaccurate. Unreliable.

hit and run
1. Swiftly attacking then retreating.
2. Failing to stop one's car after colliding, accident, etc.

hit for six Defeat resoundingly. Hit hard. Score over decisively.

hit-list Set of targets.

hit or miss [adj.] Risky in that complete success or complete failure is possible. Haphazard.

hit the hay Lie down to sleep.

hit the high spots
1. Achieve high standard of excellence.
2. Indulge in hectically enjoyable activity.

hit the road *or* **trail** Begin to travel.

hit the roof Explode with anger.

hitch [v.] Abbr. hitch-hike.

hitcher [n.] Abbr. hitch-hiker.

hitched Married.

hit man Paid assassin or ruffian.

hiya How are you?

hobo Tramp.

Hobson's choice No choice at all.

hock, in In pawn. In prison. In debt.

hog
1. [n.] Greedy, ill-mannered person.
2. [v.] Take possession of an excessive quantity of.

hog, go the whole Do something thoroughly.

hog-wash Nonsense.

hoick [v.]
1. Throw.
2. Lift.

hokey Prison.

hokey pokey
 1. Nonsense.
 2. Deceit.

hokum False sentiment.

hold down
 1. Retain in spite of difficulties.
 2. **hold down a job** Be employed.

hold everything! Wait!

hold hard Wait a moment.

hold it Refrain from movement.

hold on Wait.

hold on by the eyebrows *or* **eyelashes** Same as **hang on by one's eyebrows**.

hold one's hand Remain available to help or encourage one.

hold one's horses Delay taking action (usu. temporarily).

hold out on Keep back information, etc., from.

hold the baby See **holding**.

hold the fort Remain in charge.

hold with, not to Disapprove of.

hold your whis(h)t Be silent.

holding the baby Carrying the responsibility (usu. disagreeable). Left in charge. Usu. **leave one holding the baby**.

hole
 1. Awkward situation.
 2. Sexual intercourse.
   ● *A bit of hole.*
 3. Abbr. **arse-hole**.
 4. Untidy, squalid, unattractive place.

hole up
 1. Hide.
 2. Stay (usu. unwillingly).

holler [v.] Yell.

hols Holidays. [Juv.]

holy Joe Ostentatiously pious person.

holy Moses *or* **smoke!** Excl.

holy terror Troublesome person (usu. child).

home At the conclusion.

home and dry At a safe or successful conclusion.

home, go Wear out.

home-stretch, on the In the final stages.

home, when he (it, etc.**) is at** Expression added to questions to signify emph. incomprehension (usu. facet.).
  • *Who's he, when he's at home?*

homo [n.] Homosexual.

honest to goodness *or* **God** Absolutely genuine.

honest woman of, make an Marry.

honestly! Excl. of indignation, or surprised disgust.

honey
  1. Extremely attractive and pleasant girl.
  2. Something approved of.
  3. Affectionate term of address.

honk [v.] Vomit.

honkers Drunk.

honkey-tonk [adj.]
  1. Cheap. Nasty. Of poor repute.
  2. Jangling, noisy. (Of piano, music etc.)

honour bright! Emph. asseveration.

hoo-ha Fuss. Quarrel. Argument. Noisy discussion or disturbance.

hooch Alcoholic drink, usu. of poor quality.

hood(lum) Criminal (usu. violent).

hooey Nonsense.

hoof
  1. [n.] Foot.
  2. [v.] Kick.

3. **get the hoof** Be dismissed.
4. **hoof it** Travel on foot. Dance.
5. **hoof out** Eject.

hoofer Dancer.

hook [v.] Steal.

hook it Depart immediately. Run away.

hook, off the Freed (usu. from some constraining or difficult situation).

hook, on one's own On one's own account.

hook, on the At one's mercy. At a disadvantage.

hook on to Attach oneself to.

hook, sling one's Go away.

hook up [v.] Link up (by radio, etc.).

hook-up [n.] Connexion (by radio, etc.).

hooks, take one's
1. Go away.
2. **get one's hooks into** Annex (usu. of woman monopolising a man).

hooked
1. Captivated. **hooked on** Obsessed by.
2. Seriously addicted to drugs. [Pop.]

hookey Truant.

hooray! Excl. of pleasure.

hoot, a
1. An amusing experience. (Occ. derisive.)
   - *The whole performance was a hoot.*
2. A negligible amount.
   - *I couldn't give a hoot.* I don't care in the slightest. Also **two hoots**.

hoo(t)ch Whisky. Spirits.

hooter Nose.

hoover, to To vacuum-clean.

hop
1. Stage of a journey (usu. by aircraft).
2. Abbr. for **hop on to** Board.
3. [n.] Dance.
4. See **on the hop**.
5. **hop it** Go away.
6. **hop in** *or* **out** Got in, out (e.g. of car).

hope in hell, not a No hope whatsoever.

hope(s), some! There is no chance of that.

hopping mad Very angry.

horn
1. Trumpet (usu. in jazz music).
2. **(get** *or* **have) the horn** (Experience) erection of penis.
3. **horn in** Insinuate oneself (usu. when not welcome).

horny Sexually excited. (Of men only.)

horse around Fool around.

horse of another colour Something entirely different.

horse opera Western film.

horse sense Basic common sense.

horses, hold your Wait a moment.

hot
1. Controversial in a sensational or acrimonious way.
   - *Hot issue.*
2. Very expert. Also **hot at** *or* **on**.
3. Stolen.
   - *Hot money.*
4. Lively. Modern.
   - *Hot music.*
5. See **not so hot** and **hot on**.

hot air Empty talk.

hot and strong Very forcefully.

hot dog Hot sausage between two pieces of bread.

hot for, make it Reprimand. Punish. Make things difficult for (someone).

hot, get *or* **give it someone** Receive or issue reprimand.

hot line Line of rapid communication (usually telephone) for emergency.

hot on
1. Enthusiastic about.
2. Stringently careful about.

hot potato Delicately or dangerously controversial issue.

hot rod Very fast car.

hot seat Position of responsibility. Difficult situation. Trouble.

hot stuff
1. [n.] Sexually exciting person.
2. [n.] Expert, efficient, well-informed person.
3. [n.] Outstandingly excellent thing.
4. Excl. of approval or admiration.

hot up Warm up. Increase.

hot water Trouble. Disgrace.

house, on the Free.

how See **and how!**

how come? How? Why?

how do Form of greeting.

how-do-you-do, a A state of confusion. (Also **how-d'ye-do**.)

how goes it? What has happened lately?

how goes the enemy? See **enemy**.

how the other half lives How other people (either better or worse off) live.

how's things *or* **tricks** How are you?

how's yourself? Common retort to greeting.

howler Blunder (usu. verbal and funny).

howling Conspicuous. Overwhelming.

hoy Throw.

hubby Husband.

huddle [n.] Confidential discussion.

hum
1. [v.] Smell strongly.
2. [n.] Move briskly. Be lively.
3. [n.] Stink.

humdinger Something or somebody exceptionally pleasing.

hump
1. [v.] Have sexual intercourse.*
2. [v.] Carry.
3. **the hump** Vexation. Bad temper. Depression. Unhappiness.
4. **hump yourself!** Go away!

hunch Intuitive idea. Guess or suspicion not very firmly based.

hung over, be Be suffering from the effects of heavy drinking once drunkenness has worn off.

hung up
1. Held up.
2. Entangled.
3. Annoyed. [Pop.]
4. See **hang-up**.

hunky-dory Very pleasing.

hunt, in the
1. Having a good chance.
2. **out of the hunt** Having no chance.

husky Virile.

hussif *or* **huzzy** Pocket-case containing needles, buttons, etc.

hustle [v.] Act as **hustler**.

hustler
1. Pickpocket.
2. Energetic worker (often dishonest).
3. Swindler.
4. Prostitute.
5. Salesman relying on quick talking and sharp practice.

hype
1. Vigorous campaign to publicise person or product. Also [n.].

2. Trick.
3. Drug addict.
4. **hyped up** Excited, stimulated.

I

I don't think Expression added to ironical statement to make speaker's attitude plain.

I'll be damned *or* **hanged!**
  1. Excl. of astonishment (usu. preceded by **well!**).
  2. (Followed by **if**) Emph. negation.
     • *I'll be damned if I'll pay all that money.* I certainly will not pay so much money.

I'll eat my hat! Excl. of surprise.

I'm all right, Jack Expression of satisfaction at one's own good fortune.

I say!
  1. Excl. of surprise.
  2. Prelude to statement, etc., to attract attention.

I should cocoa *or* **worry** I don't care.

ice, on In reserve. Awaiting later attention.

idea
  1. **the idea!** Excl. of surprise.
  2. **what's the big idea?** What are you doing that for? What have you in mind? (Usu. to someone behaving surprisingly.)
  3. **have no idea** Be incompetent.

idiot box Television (set). Also **idiot channel** The commercial television service.

iffy Uncertain.

ifs and buts Conditions. Reservations.

I'll say I agree.

impot Imposition. (School slang.)

-in Added to various verbs (as **love-in, sit-in**) to signify an assembly for purposes of implementing verb.

in
1. Same as **inboard**.
2. In fashion. **the in-thing** That which is fashionable. **the in-word** The latest fashionable catch-word or -phrase.

in a spot In difficulty.

in a stew Worried. Harassed. In trouble.

in a way To a limited extent. To a certain degree.

in aid of ? what's it What is its purpose? Why has it happened?

in all my born days In all my life. [Emph.]

in-and-out Sexual intercourse.

in-crowd Clique adhering to particular fashion (e.g. in opinions, tastes, etc.).

in for Likely to have.

in for it Likely to have trouble.

in full rig Formally dressed.

in harness Employed.

in it In trouble. Also **nothing (not much** etc.**) in it** Little difference.

in-laws Relations acquired by marriage.

in point of fact Actually.

in the bag Certain. Secured.

in the cart In difficulty or disgrace.

in the clear Innocent.

in the know In possession of information or knowledge.

in the pink In good health.

in the red In debt.

in the soup In difficulties.

in the wars Injured.

in with On friendly terms with.

inboard Safe. Successful. Lucky. Usu. **I'm** (etc.) **inboard** I'm successfully catered for.

influence, under the Drunk.

innards
1. Same as **inner man**.
2. Inside workings of machinery.

inner man Stomach.

inside In prison.

inside job Crime (e.g. theft) committed by someone working or living on the premises.

intercom Intercommunication system.

into Having reached a phase when one enjoys or understands something. Usu. **be into**.
• *He's into Stravinsky at the moment.* [Pop.]

into the middle of next week Very violently. Usu. **knock someone . . .**

invite [n.] Invitation.

Irish
1. Nonsensical (usu. having to do with the opposite of what is expected).
2. Bad temper.

irk See **erk**.

iron rations Emergency rations. Simple food.

irons See **eating**.

-ism Belief, philosophy, doctrine (ex words ending in -ism).

issue, the (whole) Everything.

it
1. Very loosely used for any sexual organ or encounter, in numerous expressions and innuendos.
2. The best.

it all depends [Abbr.] It all depends on the circumstances.

itsy-bitsy Insubstantial.

itchy feet, have Be ambitious for promotion.

ivories
1. Piano keys. **tickle the ivories** Play the piano.
2. Billiard balls.
3. Teeth. **rinse one's ivories** Drink (usu. alcoholic liquor).

J

jab [n.] Inoculation.

jack
1. [n.] Policeman.
2. [v.] **jack it (in)** Cease. Stop doing it. Abandon it.
3. **on one's Jack (Jones)** Alone.
4. **jack up** Abandon. Improve.

jackpot
1. Chief prize.
2. **hit the jackpot** Be very lucky (often financially).

jag
1. Drinking bout. Usu. **on a jag** Revelry.
2. Jaguar car. See **gin**.

jail-bird Frequent or hardened prisoner.

jakes Lavatory.

jalop(p)y Old car (usu. of low value).

jam
1. [n.] Difficulty. Awkward situation. Usu. **in a jam**.
2. **jam on it** Luxury in addition to good fortune.
3. See **money for jam**.

jam full *or* **packed** Very full or tightly packed.

jam session Performance of jazz.

jam tomorrow Well-being deferred (usu. indefinitely).

jammy Fortunate.

jankers Punishment. Usu. **on jankers** Doing punishment.

jar Glass (usu. of beer).

jaw
1. [v.] Talk (excessively). Rebuke. Lecture.
2. [n.] Excessive talk. **hold one's jaw** Be quiet.
3. [n.] Impudence.

jaw-breaker Difficult word to pronounce. [adj.] **jaw-breaking** Difficult to pronounce.

jawing, give one a Reprimand one. Attempt to persuade at length.

jay-walker One who walks in the road regardless of traffic.

jazz, all that All that sort of thing (usu. slightly derog.). Deception.

jazz up Liven up. Decorate flashily. Improve or modernise.

jazzy Flashily colourful.

jell See **gel**.

jelly See **gelly**.

Jenny Lea Tea.

Jenny Wren Wren.

Jericho, to go Go to hell.

jerk Contemptible person.

jerk into it, put a Act more vigorously.

jerk (off) Masturbate.

jerks
1. Delirium tremens.
2. Physical exercises.

Jerry [n.] & [adj.] German.

jerry Chamber-pot.

Jessie Effeminate man.

Jesus wept! Excl. of anger or sorrow.

jet
1. [v.] Travel in jet aircraft.
2. **jet in** Arrive in one.
3. **jet out** Depart in one.

jet-lag Fatigue or temporal disorientation created by rapid travel (usu. by jet-plane) between countries.

jet-set Wealthy social clique frequenting international playgrounds.

Jew boy Young Jewish male. [Derog.]

jiff(y)
1. Short time.
2. **just a jiffy** Please wait a moment.
3. **in a jiffy** Shortly.

jig-(a-)jig [n.] & [v.] Sexual intercourse.

jiggered, be Be astonished. (Usu. excl. of surprise.)
● *Well I'm jiggered. I'll be jiggered.*

jiggery-pokery
1. Underhand scheming.
2. Nonsense.

jiggle Fiddle. Rearrange.

jim-jams
1. Nervous tension, excitement, fear.
2. Pyjamas. [Juv.]

jiminy! Excl. of surprise.

Jimmy riddle [n.] Urination. Also [v.].

jingle [n.] Brief song accompanying television advertisement.

jingo!, by Excl.

jink
1. [v.] Make a quick movement of aircraft to avoid being hit by fire. Also [n.].
2. [adj.] **jinking.**

jinx
1. Curse. Bringer of bad luck.
2. **put a jinx on** Make susceptible to bad luck.

jitterbug
1. Kind of dance. Also [v.].
2. Very nervous person.

jitters, the State of fear, excitement or tension [adj.] **jittery** Experiencing such tension.

jive Species of dance and dance-music [n.] **jiver** One dancing thus.

joanna *or* **joanner** Piano.

job
1. Piece of criminal activity.
2. **on the job** Having sexual intercourse.
3. See **put-up job**.
4. **just the job** Exactly what is required.
5. **make a clean job of something** Do it thoroughly.
6. **jobs for the boys** Jobs given through influence or nepotism, regardless of merit or need.

Jock
1. Scotsman.
2. Frequent term of address to Scotsman.

jock-strap Tightly-fitting piece of male underwear to support private parts (usu. in sporting activity).

Joe
1. American soldier.
2. One who is given all the dull and uninteresting jobs.

Joe Soap I (usu. in circumstances of discontent at being over-burdened).
● *I suppose Joe Soap'll have to do it.* I suppose I'll have to do it (as usual!).

john Lavatory.

John Bull Personification of England.

John O'Dreams Absent-minded, dreamy, unpractical person.

John Thomas Penis.

johnny
1. Person.
2. Dandy.
3. Condom.
4. **johnny-come-lately** Newly arrived person, therefore inex-perienced.

joint
1. Building. Place (usu. of entertainment). (Sometimes derog.)
2. Marijuana cigarette.

joke is on, the The plot, hoax, etc., has recoiled on.

joker Fellow.

joking, you must (*or* **have to) be** I don't agree with you. Gen. excl. of incredulity.

jolly
1. Coax (a depressed or reluctant person or thing into better circumstances). Usu. **jolly along** *or* **up**.
2. Very.

jolly D Good. Very kind.

jolly well Most certainly.

jordan Chamber-pot.

josh [v.] Tease.

josser Fellow.

jove!, (by) Excl. of mild surprise.

joy Luck, success (as in **any joy? no joy**, etc.).

joy-ride Car-ride (usu. at high speed and/or illegally, for pleasure only).

joy-stick Control column of aircraft.

judy Young woman.

jug
1. Poison.
2. Gaol.
3. Drink of beer. **jugged up** Well plied with beer.

jug-ears Person with ears that stick out.

juggins Fool.

juice
1. Petrol. **step on the juice** Drive faster.
2. Electric current.

juicy Salacious.

jump
1. See **high jump**.

2. [n.] A slight fright.
- *You gave me a jump.* Also [v.].
- *You made me jump.* You gave me a slight fright. Also **the jumps**.

3. [v.] Rob. Arrest.

4. **See how the cat jumps** Wait for events before committing oneself.

jump in the lake, go and Go away.

jump on Blame, criticise sharply.

jump-suit Tightly fitting suit (or trousers and matching upper garment), male or female.

jump the gun Be premature. Start ahead of time.

jump to it Hasten. Start work immediately. [Emph.]

jumped-up Conceited. Brashly successful or ambitious.

jumping-off point Starting place.

jungle-juice Strong, cheap spirits.

jungle-telegraph Same as **bush telegraph**.

junk Any narcotic drug (usu. heroin).

junkie *or* **-y** Drug addict.

Jupiter! Excl.

just Indeed.
- *Will you tell him? Won't I just!*

just fancy! Excl. of surprise or delight.

just one of those things Something that happens which has to be accepted.

just the job Exactly what is needed.

just what the doctor ordered Exactly what is necessary. Very much to be approved of.

juve Abbr. Juvenile lead. Actor playing young male leading part in theatre. Role of this kind.

K

kahsi Lavatory. Also **carsey**.

kangaroo court Illegal court (e.g. of prisoners or workmen 'trying' one of their fellows) where justice is improbable.

kaput Finished. Out of order (usu. of machinery).

kecks Pants.

keen on Attached to. Fond of. Interested in.

keep body and soul together Survive.

keep cave Act as sentinel. [Juv.]

keep down Same as **hold down**.

keep in with Remain on friendly terms with.

keep it, you can I do not want it.

keep one guessing Keep one in uncertainty.

keep one's (big) mouth shut Refrain from talking indiscreetly.

keep one's breath to cool one's porridge Refrain from interfering. Remain silent.

keep one's cool Remain unflustered.

keep one's end up Do one's share of work, etc. Sustain one's position or opinions.

keep one's eyes peeled *or* **skinned** Remain alert or watchful.

keep one's hair on Keep calm.

keep one's mouth shut Keep something secret.

keep one's pecker up Remain (or try to remain) cheerful in adversity.

keep one's shirt on Keep one's temper.

keep one's weather eye open Watch carefully.

keep tabs on Maintain careful watch on.

keep (start) the ball rolling Maintain (gain) impetus.

keep the pot boiling Earn enough to live on.

keep up with the Joneses Remain equal in social standing or material possessions with one's neighbours.

keeps, for To keep as one's own. For ever.

kerfuffle [n.] Fuss. Panic. Confusion. Uproar. Controversy. Scuffle. Disturbance.

khyber (pass) Posterior.

kibosh Bring to a stop. Spoil. Prevent. Usu. **put the kibosh on**.

kick
  1. [n.] Strong sense of satisfaction or excitement. Thrill.
  2. [v.] Abandon.
     ● *Kick a habit.*
  3. **get a kick out of** Derive a thrill from.

kick(-)back Payment in return for favours received or services rendered (usu. underhand or illegal).

kick in the pants Crude and vigorous reproof. Set-back.

kick-off Start. **for a kick-off** In the first place.

kick out Eject. Dismiss.

kick the bucket Die.

kick up a row *or* **shindy (shindig)** Create a disturbance.

kick up one's heels Enjoy oneself uninhibitedly.

kick upstairs Promote to a position which has more status but less influence.

kicks, for Purely for the sake of excitement (often of selfish or dubious nature).

kid
1. Informal term of address.
2. Brother or sister. Also **kid brother** *or* **sister**.
3. **our kid** My brother/sister.
4. Child. Also **kiddy, kiddie**.
5. [v.] Deceive. Trick. Delude. Also **kid on**. Pretend.
6. See **no kidding**.
7. **kid's stuff** Something easy or elementary.

kill Same as slay.

killing
1. Very funny. Also **killingly funny**.
2. Exhausting. Causing pain.
   • *My feet are killing me.*
3. **make a killing** Make much money from a deal. Enjoy a success.

kind of Somewhat like. Also **kinda**.

king Expert at a particular undertaking.

king-size(d) Very big.

kingdom come Eternity.

kinky Warped. Perverted. (Of person's mentality, tastes, etc.) Unusual.

kip [n.] & [v.] Sleep. **kip down** Go to bed.

kipper Term of facet. affectionate address.

kiss of death Support which will prove damaging.

kisser Mouth.

kite Aircraft.

kitsch
1. Junk.
2. [adj.] Rubbishy.

kittens, have Be in an agitated and worried state about something.

Kiwi New Zealander.

knackered Exhausted. Worn out. Finished.

knackers*
1. Testicles.
2. Excl., used in some abusive expressions, e.g.
   - *Knackers to that*. I will have none of that.

knapper Head.

knee [v.] Strike with the knee (usu. in stomach or testicles).

knee high to a grasshopper Very small.

knees-up [n.] Lively party.

knee-trembler Sexual intercourse while standing.

knickers! Excl. Also **knickers to that!** (etc.) Excl. of contempt.

knickers in a twist, have one's Be in a state of agitation.

knife, before one can say Very quickly.

knife, that one could cut with a Very noticeable.
   - *Tension that one could cut with a knife.*

knob
1. Penis.
2. Head.
3. Important person (facet. or derog).
4. See **with knobs on**.

knock
1. [n.] Innings.
2. [v.] Surprise, shock, overwhelm.
3. **take a knock** Suffer a loss (usu. financial).
4. Criticise adversely. Hence **knocking-copy** Advertisement which criticises a rival product; newspaper article of outspoken criticism.

knock-about Vigorously and noisily comic.

knock all of a heap Overwhelm with surprise.

knock back
1. Drink.
2. Cost.
   - *The evening knocked him back a few pounds.*
3. Disconcert.

knock cold
1. Render unconscious.
2. Astonish greatly.
   • *The film's knocking people cold.* The film is enjoying great success.

knock-down [adj.] Much reduced (of prices etc.).

knock for six Defeat. Surprise greatly.

knock hell out of Punish. Defeat. Damage.

knock it off! Be quiet! Don't talk nonsense! Stop it!

knock into the middle of next week Defeat. Render unconscious with a blow. Knock down vigorously.

knock off
1. Complete (usu. with ease).
2. Steal.
3. Arrest.
4. Commit (a crime).
5. Have sexual intercourse with.
6. See **knock it off!**

knock one's block off Strike one on the head (usu. facet. threat).

knock out Make in a hurry.

knock out [v.] Overwhelmingly surprise.

knock-out [n.] Overwhelmingly surprising person or thing.

knock sideways Disconcert.

knock spots off Be far superior to. Defeat easily.

knock up
1. Earn.
2. Have sexual intercourse with.
3. Make pregnant.

knocker
1. One who criticises habitually.
2. **on the knocker** On credit.

knockers Female breasts.

knocking Criticism.

knocking shop Brothel.

knots, at a (great) rate of Very quickly.

knotted! get Expression of refusal or disagreement. Also used in numerous expressions to indicate rebuff (usu. facet.), e.g.
• *He can go and get knotted.* I refuse to have anything to do with him in this matter.

know
1. In numerous expressions, e.g.
• *know the ropes, one's way around, the time of day, how many beans make five, a thing (trick) or two, what's what, which way the wind blows, one's onions* Be well-informed, efficient, alert, worldly-wise.
2. See **not that I know of**.

know-how Knowledge. Understanding.

know, in the Having information about something specific.

know whether one is coming or going, not to Be agitated, in a muddle.

knuckle down to Begin (a task, usu. reluctantly because unpleasant).

knuckle, near the Verging on the indecent. Tactlessly direct.

knuckle sandwich [n.] Punch with fist.

kook Fool.

kooky Strange. Idiotic.

kosher Genuine. Fair. Acceptable.

kraut [n.] & [adj.] German. [Derog.]

kudos Credit. Good reputation.

kyber See **khyber**.

kybosh See **kibosh**.

kyf Same as **crumpet**.

L

la-di-da Exaggeratedly mannered, apparently affected, in speech (or clothes, behaviour, etc.).

lacing Severe reprimand. Punishment.

lad Gay, amusing, irresponsible fellow. Also **a bit of a lad**.

lads Men. Usu. **the lads** Team, group etc. of men.

laddy *or* **-ie** Term of supercilious address to younger male.

lady
1. Wife. Mother. Often **the (my) old lady**.
2. **good lady** *or* **lady wife** Wife.

Lady Muck See **Lord Muck**.

lag Convict.

laid
1. See **lay**.
2. **get laid** Have sexual intercourse.

laid-back Relaxed. Suave. Unconcerned.

laid off Temporarily unemployed.

laid on Arranged.

lam
1. Thrash.
2. **lam into** Hit out at.
3. **lamming** Thrashing.

lamb turning to mutton Person experiencing advancing age.

land with Compel to shoulder unwanted responsibility.

language Swearing.

lap up Eagerly or easily absorb.

lardy dah See **la-di-da**.

large as life (and twice as natural) Plainly visible.

lark
1. [n.] Joke.
2. [v.] Amuse oneself (usu. with mischief). Usu. **lark about**.

larn Teach by punishment.

larrup [v.] Thrash. [n.] **larruping**.

lash-up
1. Mess.
2. Party.

lashings Lots.

lat Latrine. Defecation.

latch on
1. Understand.
2. Attach (oneself) to.

latest, the The most up-to-date news, joke, etc.

laugh fit to bust Laugh heartily.

laugh like a drain Laugh heartily.

laugh like hell Laugh heartily.

laughing Comfortably accommodated. Fortunate. Lucky.
• *We're laughing.*

lav Lavatory.

law, the The police.

lawks! Excl.

lay
1. [n.] Girl willing to copulate.
2. [n.] Sexual intercourse.
3. [v.] Have sexual intercourse with.
4. [v.] (In football) Pass.

lay into Thrash. Reprimand.

lay it on thick *or* **with a trowel**
1. Exaggerate.
2. Flatter fulsomely.
3. Reprimand or upbraid at length or in detail.

lay low Defeat.

lay off [v.]
1. Pass the ball (in soccer).
2. Cease. Also **lay off!** Stop it!

lay on Strike (a person).

lay on the line State publicly and clearly, so that there can be no misunderstanding.

lay on to be Pretend to be.

lay (*or* put) one's shirt Wager everything.

lay one's tongue to Think of to say.

lay out Knock unconscious.

layabout Lazy or idle person.

laze
1. [v.] Spend one's time idly.
2. [n.] Idle time.

lead in one's pencil [n.] Sexual potency.

lead me to it! With pleasure.

lead, swing the
1. Avoid work.
2. Boast.
3. [n.] **lead-swinger** One who avoids work or boasts.

lead up the garden path Deceive. Impose on. Mislead.

leak [n.] Urination. Also [v.] Urinate.

lean off Stop leaning on.

lean on Exert pressure on (person).

learn Teach.

leathering Thrashing.

leathers, the Uniform of youths (usu. in gangs) possessing motor-cycles.

leave be Refrain from interfering.

leave cold Fail to impress.

leave go Relinquish hold.

leave in the air Leave unsettled.

leave it off Stop. Desist.

leave it out Desist.

leery Sly.

leftie *or* **-y** [n.] & [adj.] Communist. Extremely left-wing socialist.

leg it Walk.

leg over, get one's Have sexual intercourse.

leg-pull [n.] Piece of teasing.

leg-show Entertainment by lady-dancers waving their legs.

leg, show a Get out of bed. See also **shake a leg**.

leggo Let go.

legit Serious drama, as opposed to revue, etc. Also [adj.] (ex legitimate).

legless Drunk.

legs, get on one's hind Rise to speak.

legs, have the Be capable of going the required distance.

legs on, have the Be able to go faster than.

lemon
1. Foolish or incompetent person.
2. See **answer is a lemon**.

lend [n.] Loan.

lend wings to Cause to hurry.

less of the lip Talk less. Be less impudent.

let alone In addition to. Even more so.

let-down Disappointment.

let 'em all come! Excl. of defiance.

let off Emit wind from anus.

let off steam Behave without inhibition.

let on
1. Reveal. Admit.
2. Pretend.

let one's (back) hair down Relax. Become informal. Enjoy oneself uninhibitedly.

let-out [n.] Means of escape.

let rip Berate.

let up [v.] Diminish. Stop. Become less (severe).

let-up [n.] Pause. Breathing-space. Relaxation.

let's have (*or* be having) you Hurry up to begin.

letch
1. [v.] Behave lecherously or feel lecherous.
2. [n.] Piece of lecherous behaviour.

level See **on the level**.

level best The utmost one can do.

level pegging Keeping abreast.

lib Liberation.

lick
1. [n.] Quick wash. Coat of paint.
2. **at a (great) lick** Very quickly.
3. [v.] Defeat. Puzzle.
4. **lick and a promise** Quick wash. Hasty doing of task.

lick of the tar-brush, have a* Be of African or Asian descent.

lid Hat.

lid on it, that's put the (tin-) That's ruined everything. That's stopped it.

lie doggo Bide one's time. Remain inconspicuous.

lie-down [n.] A rest by lying down.

lie in [v.] Remain in bed late.

lie-in [n.] Longer sleep than usual.

life, bet your See **bet your boots**.

life, have the time of one's Enjoy oneself very much.

life of Riley/Reilly, the A very enjoyable life.

life, not on your Certainly not.

life of me, for the Under any circumstances (Emph. expression to strengthen verb. e.g.
• *I can't understand it for the life of me*. I just do not understand it.).

lifer Convict serving life imprisonment.

lift [v.] Steal.

lift one's elbow Drink.

lift one's little finger, not Not make the slightest effort.

light fantastic, the Dancing. Esp. **trip the light fantastic** Dance.

lightning See **greased**.

like [adv.] As it were. (Vague addition to end of sentence or phrase.)

like a shot, billy-ho *or* **-o(h), the very devil, buggery*, hell, a bat out of hell, lightning, a house on fire, hot cakes, blazes, mad, wildfire** Very quickly or successfully.

like a ton of bricks, come down (on one) Reprimand (one) severely.

like anything Vigorously. Very much. Expression adding emph.
• *I laughed like anything*.

like(ly) as not Very likely. Probably.

like crazy Very much. (General adv. phrase of emph.)

like death (warmed up), feel, be, etc. Be very unwell.

like enough Probably.

like hell!
1. Very vigorously.
   • *Run like hell!*
2. Certainly not! Also **like hell I** (etc.) **did!** I most certainly did not!

like it or lump it Enjoy it or, if not, tolerate it.

like nobody's business Emph. adv. phrase.

like so In this way.

like something the cat('s) brought in Utterly bedraggled.

like that!, I Indignant excl. meaning the opposite of what it says.

likes of, the A person or thing such as. (Often derog.)

limb, out on a In a dangerous, risky, exposed, committed, isolated position.

limehouse Coarse abuse.

limey Englishman.

limit, the (absolute, dizzy *or* **giddy)** The extremity of endurance or expectation. (Often facet.)
● *That's the giddy limit!* I have never heard anything so surprising!

limo Car.

line See **lay on the line**.

line of country Job. Special interest.

line (on), get a Find information (about).

line-shooter One who tries to impress others by talking exaggeratedly or untruthfully. See **shoot a line**.

line up [v.] Arrange. Organise.

line-up [n.] Arrangement. Array. List of names (usu. of performers in order) or items in a programme.

lip Impudence. Impertinence. (Verbal.) [adj.] **lippy**.

liquor up Drink alcoholic liquor heavily.

little bird Facet. term for actual or pretended source of information which the speaker wishes not to specify. Often **a little bird told me**.

little bit of fluff Sexually attractive woman.

little stranger Newly-born (or about to be born) baby.

little Willie Penis.

little woman, the My wife.

lit up Mildly intoxicated.

live it up Lead a merry life.

live like a lord *or* **fighting cock** Live in luxury.

livestock Fleas.

living daylights out of, knock etc. **the** Strike heavily (usu. a person).

loaded
1. Drunk.
2. Having much money.
3. Drugged.

load of, a A lot of.

load of, get a Listen to; understand.

load on, have a Be very drunk.

loads Lots.

loaf (of bread) Head. Esp. **use one's loaf** Exercise intelligence or common sense.

lobscouse Stew of meat and vegetables.

local
1. Nearest public house.
2. Local resident.

lock-up Cell in prison or police-station.

locum One taking over work temporarily from another, esp. doctor or clergy.

lollipop
1. Same as **sugar daddy**.
2. **lollipop man** Warden supervising children crossing road.
3. Short, popular piece of classical music.

lolly
1. Money.
2. [abbr.] Lollipop.

long chalk(s), by (a) By a great deal.

long face, pull a Grimace with distaste or dissatisfaction.

long johns Men's underwear with long legs (and perhaps sleeves).

long streak of misery, a Very gloomy person.

long time no see It is a long time since I saw you last.

long vac Summer holiday. (University, etc.)

longs Normal trousers, as distinct from shorts.

loo Lavatory.

look alive Hurry up.

look at me (etc.)**, to** Judging from my (etc.) appearance.

look down one's nose at Despise.

look-in Chance. Opportunity. Hope of success.

look-see, take *or* **have a** Look. Inspect.

look sharp, snappy *or* **slipp(er)y** Hurry.

look towards Drink health of. Usu. **I looks towards you!** Good health!

look who's talking Ironical or facet. response to foolish or self-satisfied talk.

loony
1. [n.] Lunatic.
2. [adj.] Crazy.
3. **loony bin** Mental hospital.

loopy Mildly crazy.

loose
1. **on the loose** Out of prison. Drinking heavily. Enjoying oneself.
2. See **screw loose**.

loot Money.

lord love a duck! Excl. of surprise.

Lord Muck Man who (perhaps wrongly) believes himself to be of consequence.

lose out Lose. Put oneself or be at a disadvantage. Be unsuccessful.

lost See **get lost**.

lounge lizard Man who preys on wealthy women. Idler in high society.

louse Disagreeable person.

louse up Spoil. Ruin. Confuse.

lousy Thoroughly bad. Disgustingly dirty. Generally unpleasant.

lousy with
1. Having lots of.
   - *He's lousy with money.*
2. Unpleasantly crowded with.
   - *The beach is lousy with trippers.*

love Affectionate term of address.

love a duck Excl. See **lord**.

love-in [n.] Gathering for the purpose of expressing philosophy and life-style based on love. [Pop.] See **-in**.

lover boy Term of address to man or youth (usu. hostile).

love of Mike!, for the Excl. of mild disgust.

love you and leave you, I must Goodbye.

lovely [n.] Very attractive woman.

loverly Lovely.

lovey-dovey [adj.] Exaggeratedly or unusually affectionate. Sentimental.

low(-)brow
1. [n.] Person with undemanding tastes in music, reading, etc.
2. [adj.] Popular (of culture, taste, etc.). See **high(-)brow**.

low-down True facts. Information.

low water, in Short of money.

lower [v.] (Of liquor) Drink.

lubricate Supply with drink.

luck of the devil Extreme luck.

lug Ear. Also **lug-hole**.

lulu
1. Attractive girl.
2. Pleasing object or event.

lumber, in (dead) In (serious) trouble.

lumbered
1. In trouble.
2. **be (get) lumbered with** Be (made) unwillingly responsible for.

lummy *or* **-e!** Excl.

lump
1. [v.] Dislike. Usu. **like it or lump it** Like it or not.
2. **the lump** System of employing workers (usu. in building-industry) on daily or temporary basis, not by permanent agreement.

lumping Ungainly. Heavy.

lush
1. Attractive (of girl).
2. [n.] Attractive boy or girl.
3. Abbr. luscious.

M

Mac(k) General term of address to Scotsmen.

McCoy, the real Excellent. A first class example of its type.

macho Aggressively masculine.

mad Also **mad at** Very annoyed with. See **get one's mad up** *or* **out**.

madam
1. Proprietress or manageress of brothel. Also **madame**.
2. (Of small girls) Sophisticated, stubborn or bad-tempered child. Usu. **proper (little) madam**.

made, have something *or* **be** Be fortunate or successful.

made of money Rich.

made up Promoted.

Mae West Lifebelt. Life-jacket.

mag Magazine.

magic Very pleasing.

magpie [adj.] Prone to collect miscellaneous objects.

main-brace, splice the Drink. Distribute drink.

mainline
1. [n.] Important vein for injection of drugs.
2. [v.] Take narcotics intravenously.

make
1. Steal. Acquire.

2. (Persuade to) have sexual intercourse with (one).

3. Catch in time (aircraft, bus, etc.).

4. **make it (together)** Copulate.

5. [n.] **on the make** Concentrating on or succeeding in making money or achieving status.

6. Secure attention or favour of one of opposite sex.

make a balls(-up) of* See **balls**.

make a day *or* **night of it** Devote whole day or night to a particular purpose.

make a go of Succeed at.

make a hole in

1. Use or complete a large portion of.

2. **make a hole in one's pocket** Cost a lot of money.

make a monkey of one make one look foolish.

make a pass at Attempt to flirt with.

make a place too hot to hold one Acquire such a reputation that one has to leave a place.

make a song and dance (about) Make a fuss (about).

make do and mend Make the best use of what one has.

make it hot for See **hot for**.

make it snappy Be brief.

make on Pretend.

make one's pile Acquire riches.

make one sit up Startle one.

make out

1. Fare.

2. Explain.
   - *How do you make that out?* What do you mean by that?

make them, as they As possible.
   - *As stupid as they make them.* Very stupid.

make tracks Go. Depart.

make tracks for Go after, towards.

make up Promote.

make with
1. Use.
2. Make.
3. Achieve sexual intercourse with.
4. Supply.

man
1. Term of address to either sex, of any age. (Usu. Pop.)
2. **old man** Boss. Father. Husband. Also informal and friendly term of address.

man of straw *or* **wax** Weak, unreliable, untrustworthy man.

man-sized Very large or difficult.

mandarin Senior or pompous civil servant.

manhandle Handle (person) roughly.

manky Nasty.

manor Police district.

map, put on the Make prominent or important.

marbles
1. Testicles.
2. **have all one's marbles** Be alert, well-informed, efficient.

marching orders Instructions. Dismissal.

marge Margarine.

marines, tell it to the I don't believe it.

mark up [v.]
1. Label.
2. Give credit for.

marry up Conform. Reconcile.

mash [v.] Brew.

massacre of the innocents Withdrawal of unpassed bills at end of parliamentary session.

mat, on the In trouble. About to be reprimanded.

mate Term of informal address, sometimes unfriendly.

matey
1. same as **mate**.
2. [adj.] Very friendly.

matric Matriculation.

mauler Hand. Fist.

maxi [adj.] Of generous dimensions. Also [n.].

me-and-you Menu. [Facet.]

mean Skilful.

mean a thing, not Be of no importance.

meany *or* **-ie** A mean person.

measly Meagre. Contemptibly inadequate.

meat wagon
   1. Ambulance.
   2. Police van.

medals showing Flies undone.

medic, medico Doctor. Medical student.

meet one's Waterloo Encounter final defeat.

menace [n.] Troublesome person.

mental [adj.] Mentally defective.

merchant Fellow. Person. (Slightly patronising). Person keen on an activity.

mere nothing, a Not worth recognition or thanks.

mess about with Deal with in an inefficient or untidy way.

message, get the Understand the point of a (sometimes indirect) warning, hint or remark. Understand a situation or point of view.

messer Bungler.

mess-up [n.] Mess.

meths Methylated spirits.

Met (Office) Meteorological Office.

Michael *See* **mickey**.

Mick(y) Irishman. Roman Catholic. (Derog.)

Mickey Finn Strong alcoholic drink.

mickey (out of), take the Make fun (of). Occ. **take the Michael**.

middle-aged spread Thickening of the waist-line with middle-age.

middle of next week See **knock**.

middling Moderately (large, well, etc.).

miffed Offended.

miffy Ready to take offence.

mike Microphone.

Mike, for the love of Excl. of irritation or despair.

miles *or* **a mile** Very considerably.

miles away Inattentive. Lost in thought.

milk-run Regular or easy task.

mind-bending [adj.] Such as to create extreme mental difficulties (in comprehending something, etc.). Also **mind-boggling**.

mind-blowing Producing ecstasy or oblivion (usu. by music, drugs, etc.). [Pop.]

mind? do you Excl. of objection.

minder Bodyguard.

mind me, don't
1. Sarcastic comment on thoughtless behaviour towards oneself.
2. Polite insistence that one will not be inconvenienced by what is proposed.

mind out! Be careful.

mind your back(s)! Move out of my way!

mind your eye Proceed with caution.

mine's Mine is. My choice of drink is.

mingy Mean. Unsatisfactorily small.

mini-
1. [adj.] Very small.
2. Abbr. for small car (occ. **minnie**), short skirt, etc.

misery Doleful or peevish person.

misery, (long) streak of Gloomy person.

mish-mash Confused state. Disorganised condition.

miss [Abbr.] Miscarriage.

miss out on Miss.

miss the bus Lose an opportunity.

miss the boat Be too late.

missus, the My wife.

mistake, and no Most certainly.

mitt Hand. Fist. Also **frozen mitt** Chilly reception. Dismissal.

mittens Handcuffs. Boxing-gloves.

mixer Trouble-maker.

mix it [v.] Fight (usu. of several people).

mixed-up Mentally or emotionally confused.

mizzle Decamp. Also **do a mizzle**.

mo Moment.

moan [n.] & [v.] Grumble.

moaner Grumbler.

mob Gang.

mockers on, put the Put an end or halt to (e.g. idea, plan). Cause interference with.

mod con(s) [Abbr.] Modern conveniences.

model of, the (very) Closely resembling.

mods
1. Teenagers or teenage-gangs with life-style attaching importance to smart clothes and motor-scooters.
2. Moderations. (The first public degree examination at Oxford.)

mog off Depart.

mog(gy) Cat. (In N. England, mouse.)

moither [v.] Irritate.

moke Donkey.

mole Spy.

moll
 1. Prostitute.
 2. Girl. (Often girl-friend of criminals.)

Molotov cocktail Incendiary device (usu. in bottle).

money for jam *or* **old rope** Money easily earned or acquired.

money, for my (etc.) As far as my (etc.) own preference is concerned.

money from a blindman, like pinching Very easy.

money, made of Rich.

monkey
 1. See **make a monkey**, and **toss, not give a monkey's**.
 2. £500.
 3. **get** *or* **put one's monkey up** Anger one. Become angry.

monkey business Underhand or foolish behaviour. Mischief.

monkey, cold enough to freeze the balls off a brass* Very cold.

monkey tricks Misbehaviour. Mischief.

monkey's (toss), not to give (care) a Not to care in the least.

monniker Name. Signature.

moo
 1. Term of address to females (usu., but not always, affectionate). Also **silly (old) moo**.
 2. [Abbr.] **moo-cow**. Cow. [Juv.]

mooch
 1. Wander or loaf aimlessly. Loiter. Walk slowly.
 2. [n.] **moocher**. One who does this.

moon, over the In raptures.

moonlight [v.] Have a job additional to one's principal occupation (sometimes kept secret for tax purposes).

moonlight flit Departure late at night with one's possessions to avoid paying rent.

moonlighter Bigamist.

moonraker
1. Smuggler.
2. Fool.

moonshine Nonsense.

Moor, the Dartmoor Prison.

mop the floor with Reprimand. Defeat easily.

mop up
1. Drink.
2. Eliminate the remains of opposition. Hence **mopping-up (operations)**. (Military.)
3. Finish.

moppet Affectionate term of address to child.

more kicks than halfpence More blame than praise.

more like
1. Nearer.
   - *Six bottles won't be enough; we'll need more like eleven.*
2. **more like (it)** More satisfactory.
   - *Six bottles? Eleven will be more like it.*

more power to your elbow Expression of encouragement.

moreish Pleasant to drink or eat, so that one wants more.

morning after the night before The effect of a previous evening's heavy drinking.

mortal Emph. adj. or adv.
- *Every mortal thing.* Absolutely everything.

mosey
1. [v.] Go. Wander. Walk aimlessly.
2. [n.] Act of doing this. Also **a mosey round** A casual visit, to look at something.

mostest Most. [Emph.]

mother's boy Pampered boy.

mother's ruin Gin.

mouldy Unattractive. Of little value. Boring.

mount [v.] Get on, for sexual intercourse.

mourning, in With dirty finger-nails.

mouse-trap Cheese (usu. cheap and popular variety).

mouth
1. Talkativeness. Impudence.
2. **mouth like the bottom of a bird- (*or* parrot-) cage** Foulness of taste following heavy drinking.
3. **put one's money where one's mouth is** Support one's opinions by action.

mouthful
1. Abuse. Usu. **get a mouthful, give one a mouthful**.
2. **say a mouthful** Say something surprising or significant.

mouth, shut your Stop talking. Also **keep one's mouth shut** Not reveal a secret.

mouth too wide, open one's Talk indiscreetly.

mouthy Impudent. Indiscreet. Talkative.

move on, get a Hurry.

movie
1. [adj.] Belonging to the cinema (e.g.
   • *movie-star*, well-known film actor or actress).
2. **movie-fiend** Frequent visitor to cinema.
3. [n.] Film. Also **the movies**.

mozzy Mosquito.

Mr Right The man one wishes to marry.

Mrs Grundy Person of conventional respectability.

Mrs Mopp Charwoman.

much of a muchness Practically identical. Indistinguishable.

muck
1. See **Lord Muck**.
2. **as muck** Extremely.
   • *Common as muck*. Very common.
3. **muck about** Inconvenience. Waste time. Behave ineffectually.

muck in [v.] Work. Share tasks. Also **muck in with** Share living-quarters and/or duties with.

muck of, make a Spoil. Make untidy.

muck out Clean (a place).

muck-raking Discussing or revealing scandalous matters of unsavoury gossip.

muck up [v.] Spoil. Make untidy. Bungle.

muck-up [n.] Muddle. Failure.

mucked about, be Be inconvenienced.

mucker
1. Friend. Companion.
2. Heavy fall.

mud in your eye! Good luck! (Toast.)

mud, one's name is One's reputation has sunk. One is disgraced.

mud-slinger Slanderer.

mud-slinging Indulging in slander.

muff [v.] Bungle.

mug
1. Face. Mouth.
2. Simpleton.
3. [v.] Attack with a view to rob.

mug up Learn for examination or for some other special purpose.

mug's game Activity or undertaking which is foolish and unlikely to be successful or profitable.

mugging [n.] Robbery with violence.

muggins
1. Simpleton. Person easily imposed on.
2. I. (Similar to **Joe Soap**.)

mugwump Foolish (or indecisive) person.

mullarkey Unacceptable behaviour, procedure, etc.

mum
1. Mother. Also **mummy**.
2. Silence.
3. **mum's the word** Say nothing.

mumbo-jumbo Nonsensical verbiage.

murder
1. See **blue murder**.
2. **get away with murder** Succeed in doing as one wishes.

murky
1. Containing discreditable or sinister secrets.
2. **murky past** Unsavoury past life (usu. facet.).

murphy Potato.

musak Popular musical fodder, esp. of type played incessantly through loud-speakers in restaurants, shops, etc.

muscle in Intrude (usu. when not welcome).

mush
1. Mouth. Face.
2. Term of address.
3. Sentimentality.
4. Companion.

mushy Sentimental.

must, a That which ought to be done, seen, etc.

mustard Keen, eager. Efficient. First-class.

mutt Simpleton.

Mutt and Jeff Two well-known comedians, who figure in several expressions having to do with comic inefficiency, etc.

mutton dressed as lamb Something inferior which has been made to appear better than it is. Often woman inappropriately dressed in style of much younger one.

mutton-head Fool. **mutton-headed** Foolish.

muvver Mother (Cockney).

muzak See **musak**.

my (giddy) aunt! Excl. of surprise.

my foot! Excl. of disbelief.

my goodness, hat, godfathers! Excl. of surprise.

my word! Excl. of surprise.

N

'n And.

nth degree, the An unspecified amount.

NBG No bloody good.

nab Seize. Arrest. Steal. Obtain.

nadgers Undiagnosed fault. **give one the nadgers** Irritate.

naff Stupid.

naff off Go away.

nail down Identify. Be precise about.

nail in one's coffin Action or event likely to impair one's reputation or success.

name (for oneself), get a Acquire a reputation (usu. bad).

name it, you No matter what.

name of the game, the The nature of the circumstances.

name, to one's In one's possession or ownership.
- *He hasn't a penny to his name.*

name in vain, take one's Mention one by name. [Facet.]

name of, in the Used in numerous expressions merely for emph.
- *What in the name of thunder is he doing?* What is he doing?

nana Foolish or feeble person.

nancy (boy) Male homosexual.

nap(per) Head.

nark
1. One who acts as informer to the police.
2. [v.] Irritate.
3. **nark it!** Be quiet! Stop it!

narked Annoyed.

narky Irritable. Sarcastic.

nasty piece of work Unpleasant person.

natch Natural. Naturally.

natter
1. [v.] Chatter, often complainingly.
2. [n.] Talk. Discussion, usu. aimless.

natural
1. [n.] One who is naturally gifted in a particular activity. An activity which is naturally suited to one.
2. **in all my natural (born days)** In all my life.

near as dammit Very nearly.

near the knuckle See **knuckle**.

neat Excellent.

necessary, the The essential cash. Anything needed for a purpose.

neck
1. [n.] Impudence. Also **brass neck** Shameless impudence.
2. [v.] Embrace amorously.
3. **get it in the neck** Be severely reprimanded. Suffer unpleasant blow.
4. **break one's neck** Hurry.
5. **by a neck** Narrowly.
6. **talk through (the back of) one's neck** Talk nonsense.
7. **pain in the neck** Disagreeable person (or thing).
8. **stick one's neck out** Take a risk. Be provocative.
9. **neck of the woods** District.
10. **up to the neck** Deeply.
11. **dead from the neck up** Unintelligent.

neddy
1. Ass.
2. Fool.

needful, the The necessary cash. Anything needed for a purpose.

needle
1. [v.] Irritate. Annoy.
2. **the needle** Irritation Esp. **get** *or* **take the needle** Become annoyed.
3. [adj.] Crucial (usu. in sporting usage, esp. *needle-match*, sometimes with implication of ill-feeling among contestants or of special passion among spectators).
4. **on the needle** Addicted to injected drugs.

nelly
1. Foolish or feeble person.
2. **not on your nelly!** Under no circumstances!

nerk Foolish or disagreeable person. Also **nerd**.

nerve, a Impudence.

nervy Impudent.

Nessie Nickname of Loch Ness monster.

nest, on the Having sexual intercourse. (Of men.)

never-never, the The hire-purchase system.

never no more Never. [Emph.]

new boy *or* **bug** New arrival, esp. employee.

new one Something never previously encountered. **new one on me** My first experience (of something identified).

news-hawk (*or* **-hound)** Newspaper reporter.

newt, pissed (tight *or* **drunk) as a** Very drunk.

next to nothing Hardly anything.

next week, knock into the middle of See **knock**.

nibble at Express cautious interest in.

nibs, his Any man of consequence. (Facet. or ironic.)

nice and Very.

nice as pie Very polite (usu. unexpectedly).

nice work! Excl. of congratulation.

nick
1. [n.] Prison. Police station.
2. [v.] Apprehend. Arrest.
3. **Old Nick** The Devil.
4. **in good nick** In good condition.
5. [v.] Steal. **on the nick** Stealing.

nicker £1.

niff
1. [n.] Unpleasant smell.
2. [n.] & [v.] Sniff.
3. [v.] Smell unpleasantly. [adj.] **niffy**.

nifty Stylish. Clever. Agile. Skilful.

nigger
1. Negro [Derog.]
2. **nigger in the woodpile** Something or someone who spoils a good thing.

niggly Irritable.

night of it, make a Spend an enjoyable evening or night in high living.

nightie *or* **-y** Night-dress.

nignog
1. Fool.
2. Coloured person. [Derog.]

ninepence, right as Recovered to good health.

nineteenth hole, the The bar in the club-house of a golf-course.

nip Go (usu. quickly). Step (usu. nimbly).

nipper Small child.

nippy
1. Quick. Brisk.
2. Chilly. Frosty.

Nips Japanese. [Derog.]

nit Simpleton. [adj.] **nitty** Foolish.

nitty-gritty, the The essentials, fundamentals, details, of a plan, project, matter, etc., as distinct from broad outlines.

nix
1. Nothing.
2. **keep nix** Keep look-out for someone's approach.

no can do I, you (etc.) cannot do that.

no chance There is no possibility of that!

no chicken Middle-aged or elderly.

no dice No success or luck.

no end
1. Very much.
2. A great number or amount.

no fear!
1. No! [Emph.]
2. **no fear of** No possibility of.

no flies on No stupidity, foolishness, inefficiency, etc., about.

no go No. No use. Also gen. expression to denote lack of success.

no-go [adj.] Forbidden (of access).

no great shakes Inferior. Unimportant.

no joy See **joy**.

no kidding Seriously. (Or interrogatively, You're not joking?)

no mistake, and For certain.

no names, no packdrill No-one will be identified by name, so that no responsibility can be individually allocated.

no nothing Nothing whatever.

no object No difficulty.

no odds It is immaterial or unimportant.

no oil painting Ugly.

no two ways about it No alternative.

no way Not at all.

nob
1. Head.
2. Person of position, rank or money.

nobble
1. Surreptitiously interfere with a race-horse (e.g. using drugs) before a race.
2. Steal.
3. Buttonhole. Seize. Appropriate. Attempt to influence (person).

nobody's business Something so alarming that it does not bear speculating about.

nod is as good as a wink (to a blind donkey), a A hint is worth taking note of.

nod, on the
1. On credit.
2. Without discussion; as a mere formality.

noddle Head.

noggin Simpleton.

nohow In no way.

non-starter Something which will not succeed or work.

nonsense of, make a Spoil. Make no sense.

nope No.

north and south Mouth.

nose-bag, put on the Eat (usu. hurriedly).

nose, get up someone's Annoy.

nose in, put *or* **shove one's** Interfere in an unwelcome way.

on the nose Precisely.

nose out of joint, put one's Offend one.

nose-rag Handkerchief.

nosey Inquisitive.

nosey parker Inquisitive person.

nosh
1. [n.] Food. Meal.
2. [v.] Eat.
3. **have a nosh-up** Eat (usu. quite lavishly).

nostrils, get up one's Irritate one extremely.

nosy See **nosey**.

not a bean No money at all.

not a bit (of it) Not at all. (Polite acknowledgement of thanks.)

not a patch on Very inferior to.

not a pin to choose between Equal.

not a sausage Nothing.

not all there Mentally deficient.

not an earthly (chance) No chance whatever.

not cricket Not fair.

not done *or* **not the done thing** Not what is socially or normally accepted.

not for all the tea in China In no circumstances whatsoever.

not fussy Indifferent, verging on antipathetic.

not half
 1. [adv.] Very much.
 2. Excl. of emph. agreement.

not having any *or* **that** Refusing to accept, believe, etc.

not if I know it Emph. negative.

not likely! Certainly not!

not much cop Not much use or value.

not much of a . . . Not a . . . to any great extent.

not on your life *or* **nelly** Certainly not.

not so dusty
 1. Quite good.
 2. Not very good.

not so hot Not very satisfactory.

not the foggiest (notion) No knowledge whatever.

not to worry! Do not concern yourself!

not worth a bean, button, curse, fart,* monkey's toss,* tinker's curse (etc.) Worthless.

nothing doing No. [Emph.]

nothing on earth, feel *or* **look like** Feel or look ill; look ugly.

nothing on, have
1. Be in no way superior to.
2. Have no grievance against.
3. Be free of social engagements. Be unoccupied.

nothing to make a song and dance about Not worth mentioning.

nothing to write home about Insignificant.

now you're talking! At last you are saying something which interests me or with which I can agree.

nowhere, be Be severely defeated.

nowhere, in the middle of In a remote spot.

nozzle Nose.

nuff said The discussion is ended. I agree. Enough has been said.

number [n.] Dress. See **opposite number**.

number is up, one's One is dead or dying, in serious trouble.

number one
1. Oneself. One's own interests.
2. First Lieutenant (Royal Navy).
3. Best uniform or clothes.
4. See **ones**.

number up, have one's Be dead, dying or in serious trouble.

numbers, by In an orderly way.

nut
1. Head. Also **off one's nut** Mad.
2. Foolish person. (Abbr. **nut-case**.)
3. Person (usu. troublesome) (e.g.
   ● *tough nut.*).
4. [v.] Butt. Also **put the nut on**.
5. [n.] Fanatic.

nut-case Daredevil. Foolish or mad person. (Usu. emph. derog.)

nut, do one's Be or become very angry.

nut-house Lunatic asylum.

nuts
1. [adj.] Mad. Usu. **nuts about** Enthusiastic about.
2. [n.] Testicles.
3. **nuts on** Devoted to. Keenly interested in.
4. **be dead nuts on** Be very fond of.
5. **can't do something for nuts** Can't do it well.
6. Exclamation of derision. Also **nuts to you, him** etc.

nuts and bolts Basics. Essentials.

nutter Same as **nut-case**.

nutty
1. Crazy.
2. **nutty on** See **nuts on**.
3. **nutty as a fruit cake** Very crazy.

nympho Nymphomaniac.

O

OK All right.

OK by me Agreeable to me.

oats, earn one's Deserve one's keep.

oats, off one's Without appetite.

object [n.] Contemptible or absurd person.

obstropulous Obstreperous (Various spellings).

oceans of A lot of.

odd-ball Unusual or eccentric person. Also [adj.].

odd bod
1. Person who isn't doing anything and who is thus available for a task.
2. Same as **odd fish**. See **bod**.

odd fish Unusual type of person.

odds and sods Miscellaneous persons or things of no special importance or function.

off
1. Unfit for consumption.
2. Unwell.
3. Not up to one's usual standard.
4. Unacceptable. Usu. **a bit off**.
   - *I thought his attitude was a bit off.*
5. Without interest in.
6. No longer on the menu.

off-beat Unconventional.

off one's back See **back**.

off one's chest No longer preoccupying one or weighing on one's spirits.

off one's food *or* **feed** Suffering from loss of appetite.

off one's head *or* **nut** Mad.

off one's oats Indisposed. Without appetite.

off one's rocker Mad.

off-putting Discouraging. Disconcerting.

off the beam Wrong. Thinking along incorrect lines.

off the deep end See **deep end**.

off the hook, (let one) (Allow one) freedom from a threat, punishment, stress or strain, constraint, etc.

off the top Spontaneously. Without fore-thought.

oggin River, canal, sea.

oh boy! *or* **my!** Excl.

oh yeah? I don't believe you, it, etc.

oick Unpleasant person.

oil painting, no Ugly.

oil, strike Be lucky.

oil the knocker Tip the porter.

oiled
1. Semi-intoxicated.
2. **well oiled** Drunk.

oils Waterproof clothing.

okey-doke Same as **OK**. Also **okey-dokey**.

old
1. Gen. adj. prefix (usu. in terms of address) indicating affectionate familiarity or cordiality, and having no connexion with age. Also **good old**.
2. In other slang expressions, can be derog. adj. See below.

old-and-bitter Mother-in-law.

old battleaxe Domineering (sometimes unpleasant) woman of formidable voice, deportment and attitude.

old bean Term of familiar address.

old Bill Police. Policeman.

old bird Experienced person.

old boy
1. Familiar term of address.
2. **the old boy** The boss.

old boy net(work) Useful social or business connexions formed by friends, often by former pupils of the public schools.

old buffer See **buffer**.

old chap Term of address.

old crock Decrepit thing (usu. very old car). Decrepit person.

old dear
1. Elderly and agreeable woman.
2. Term of address. [Facet.]

old dutch See **Dutch**.

old-fashioned look Critical, knowing or disapproving look.

old fogey Person with old-fashioned or fixed tastes, views, attitudes, etc.

old fruit Term of address. [Facet.]

old gang Elderly and reactionary members in society, organisation, etc.

old girl
1. Familiar term of address.
2. Wife. Mother.
3. Former pupil of a school.

old guard Same as **old gang**.

old hand Experienced person.

old Harry The devil.

old Harry, play Make havoc, uproar, discomfort.

old hat [adj.] Out of date. Tediously well-known.

old how, any Any how.

old lad Familiar term of address.

old man
1. Term of address.
2. Father. Husband.
3. **the old man** One's superior, boss, etc.

old Nick See **nick (3)**.

old soldier Experienced person. Also **come the old soldier over** Lay claim to superior wisdom and more experience than.

old son Affectionate term of address.

old sport Term of familiar address (rather old f.).

old stick, funny Rather puzzling, unapproachable person.

old sweat Experienced person, often soldier.

old thing Familiar term of address.

old thing, any Anything.

old trout Disagreeable woman.

old woman Wife. Mother.

olde worlde Facet. adj. phrase to describe self-conscious attempt at creating artificially an appearance or atmosphere of the past.

oldie Old film or song. Also **golden oldie** Good old film, song etc.

on
1. Creating disadvantage for. (In numerous expressions, e.g.
   - *The car broke down on me.*)
2. Willing and ready.
   - *Are you on?*
3. Possible.
   - *It's just not on.*
4. Payable by.
   - *The drinks are on me.*
5. Wagered on.
   - *We'll have £1 on the favourite.*

on about, go *or* **be** Grumble about. Speak at length or incomprehensibly about.

on at, be Nag.

on, go Speak at length. Last a long time.

on one's back See **back**.

on one's own
1. Alone.
2. On one's own initiative. By one's own efforts.

on spec As a speculation. Taking a risk.

on the beer Indulging in heavy drinking.

on the dot (of) Punctually (at).

on the go Moving about.

on the ground floor At the beginning, or at the lowest level, of an enterprise that has possibilities of profit or success.

on the hop Unawares.

on the house Free.

on the level Fair. Honest, with no reservations.

on the nod Without discussion.

on the up and up Getting steadily better or more successful.

on the (water) waggon Abstaining from alcoholic drink.

on tick On credit.

on to Fully aware of.

once-over General examination (usu. quick and superficial).

oncer £1 note.

one
1. [n.] Blow.
   - *She fetched him one.* She hit him.
2. [n.] Lie.
   - *That's a big one.*
3. [n.] Amusing person.
   - *You are a one!*
4. Drink.
   - *A quick one.*
5. Joke.
   - *Have you heard the one about . . . ?*

one-armed bandit Slot-machine for gambling.

one better, go Do better (than something previously referred to).

one born every minute, there's Said as comment on idiotic action by someone, often oneself.

one for, a (real) A devotee of or enthusiast for.

one for the road A final drink before leaving.

one-horse [adj.] Inferior. Of low quality.

one in every village, there's Said as comment on idiotic action by someone.

one in the eye A snub, setback, rebuff, rebuke.

one of the best See **best, one of the**

one of the lads A genial and companionable fellow.

one of those A homosexual.

one of those things Something that happens and has to be tolerated.

one-off [adj.] Single. Usu. **one-off job** Task or undertaking different and distinct from others and not to be repeated.

one or two, have had Be slightly drunk.

one over the eight, have had Be drunk.

one too many, have had Be drunk.

one-track mind Mind obsessed with sex, or with some other consuming interest.

one-two, a (or** the old)** Two quick blows.

one up on, be Have gained an advantage over.

ones, do Urinate. Also **do number ones**.

onions, know one's Be efficient, alert, experienced.

onions, off one's Crazy.

oodles Large quantities.

oojah Gen. term for any object of which one does not know, or has forgotten, the name.

oomph Sex appeal. Enthusiasm.

oops-a-daisy! Sympathetic excl. (usu. when someone falls, slips, or drops something, etc.).

op
1. [Abbr.] Opus, a musical work.
2. [Abbr.] Surgical operation.

open and shut case Matter simple to resolve, there being no need for much investigation or further evidence.

open one's mouth too wide Talk indiscreetly.

oppo(site number) Person of equivalent rank, status, position, etc., in another institution, business, branch of a large concern, etc. Friend. Colleague.

optic [n.] Eye.

or else Emph. threat with ominous but undefined penalties implied.

order of the boot Dismissal.

order, tall Stiff requirement. Difficult undertaking.

organ-grinder, not the monkey, the The chief person, not his subordinate.

organise a piss-up in a brewery, not be able to* Be inefficient.

ornery Of poor quality.

orter Ought to.

other pebbles on the beach Alternative opportunities available.

other way about Opposite.

out
1. Unfashionable.
2. Inaccurate.

out-and-outer Whole-hearted enthusiast.

out for Specially concentrating on.

out like a light, go Fall suddenly and deeply asleep. Faint without warning.

out of commission Not functioning.

out of the hunt Having no further chance of success.

out of this world Superlatively good.

out on one's ear, thrown (etc.) Emph. form of 'thrown out'.

out with it Tell me.

outfit Group. Organisation.

outside, at the At the most. At the highest calculation.

outside of, get Eat. Drink.

over the hill Past one's best. Elderly.

over the sticks Steeplechasing.

over the top, go Exaggerate. Melodramatise. Go too far. Make oneself appear foolish by over-statement.

overboard (on), go Be wildly enthusiastic (about).

overkill [n.] Unnecessarily strong or savage action or reaction.

overstep the mark Exceed the accepted limits.

own back See **get one's own back**.

own goal, score an Make a mistake damaging to oneself.

own up Confess.

ownsome, on one's Alone.

P

Ps and Qs, mind one's Exercise care in behaviour.

PDQ Promptly. (Abbr. Pretty Damn Quickly.)

pack a punch Have a powerful effect.

pack in Finish. Also same as **pack up**.

pack it in *or* **up** End it.

pack up Go out of action. Stop working or functioning.

packet
  1. Large amount (of money).
  2. Serious trouble. (See below.)

packet, stop (get, cop, catch) a Run into serious trouble. Be severely reprimanded. Be injured.

pad Living quarters, esp. bed(-room).

pad it Walk.

paddy
  1. Bad temper. Rage.
  2. Irishman.
  3. **paddy-waggon** Police van.

paid to, put End. Deal with effectively.

pain in the arse* *or* **neck** Something or someone objectionable, irritating, boring. Also **he gives me a pain in the arse*** I find him objectionable, etc.

paint the town red Enjoy oneself hugely.

pair of spectacles Two innings without scoring. (Cricket.)

Paki Pakistani. [Derog.] Also **Paki-bashing** Criminal assault on Pakistanis.

pal
1. Friend. Mate.
2. **pal up with** Become friendly with.
3. [adj.] **pally** Informally friendly.

palaver Fuss and bother. Affair.

pan
1. [n.] Face.
2. [v.] Criticise very strongly.

pan, down the Same as **down the drain**.

pan out Eventuate.

pancake [v.] Land vertically while level. (Of aircraft.)

panic stations A state of alarm, bustle, confusion.

pansy Dandified, effeminate man. Homosexual male.

panto Pantomime.

pants down, with one's Unprepared, usu. in embarrassing circumstances.

pants off, bore the Bore extremely.

pants off, frighten the Frighten severely.

pants off one, have *or* **take the** Reprimand severely.

pants off, talk the Talk excessively.

paper [v.] Fill a theatre with audience admitted with free tickets. Usu. **paper the house**.

paper over the cracks Conceal deficiencies, weaknesses, disagreements.

para [Abbr.]
1. Paragraph.
2. Paratrooper.

paralytic Drunk.

park
1. Football field.
2. [v.] Place.
   • *Park yourself in that chair.*

parky Very chilly.

parlour tricks Minor social accomplishments.

parrot-cage, have a mouth like the bottom of a See **bird-cage**.

partic Particular.

pash Same as **crush**.

pass at, make a Make advances to (person of the opp. sex).

pass, I I do not wish to say (or do) anything.

pass out Faint. Become unconscious.

pass round the hat Collect money from a body of people for specific purpose.

pass the baby *or* **buck** *or* **can** Shift responsibility from oneself to someone else.

passenger Incompetent member of team, organisation, etc.

past it Too old.

past praying for Worn out. Valueless. Hopeless.

paste [v.] Thrash. [n.] **pasting**.

patch Police district. One's home ground or area of personal responsibility.

patch on, not a Not as good as.

Paul Pry Inquisitive person.

paw
 1. [n.] Hand.
 2. [v.] Handle unnecessarily, clumsily or unpleasantly.

pay off [v.] Prove successful.

pay-off
 1. [n.] Final settlement. Climax.
 2. [adj.] Final.

pay out Be revenged on.

pay the earth Pay a very large sum of money.

payola Payment of money for favours received (usu. illegal or underhand).

pea-shooter Gun.

pea-souper Dense fog.

peach
1. [n.] Attractive person. Thing having merit, worth. [adj.] **peachy**.
2. [v.] Reveal incriminating secrets.

peanuts A trivial matter (usu. an insignificant amount of money).

pearly gates Entrance to heaven.

peas and cues see **ps and qs**.

pebble on the beach, not the only Not the only available or desirable person or thing.

pecker up, keep one's Remain (or try to remain) cheerful or brave in adversity.

peckish Hungry.

pee
1. [v.] Urinate.
2. [n.] Urination. Also **pee-pee**.
3. **pee oneself** Laugh heartily.

peel undress.

peeled, keep one's eyes Keep a careful look-out.

peep [v.] Sound the horn of a car. Also [n.] **give (it) a peep** Blow the horn. **give him** (etc.) **a peep** Warn him by blowing horn.

peepers Eyes.

peeved Irritated. Offended. Annoyed.

peg
1. Wooden leg.
2. Cricket stump.
3. Penis.*
4. [v.] Throw (stone).
5. [n.] Leg.

peg-leg Wooden leg(ged man).

peg out
1. Die.
   - *I'm pegging out for a drink.* I would very much like a drink.
2. End. Stop.

peggy Tooth. [Juv.]

peke Pekinese dog.

pelt [v.] Hurry.

pen-pusher Clerk. Bureaucrat.

pencil, lead in one's Sexual potency.

penguin suit White tie and tails.

penn'orth Pennyworth.

penny for them (*or* your thoughts), (a) Expression addressed to silent, obviously preoccupied person, inviting him to confide.

penny has dropped Point has been understood.

penny numbers, in In small quantities.

people Relatives.

pep
1. Energy.
2. **pep up** Invigorate. Inspire.
3. **pep-pill** Stimulant pill.
4. **pep-talk** Encouraging address.

perc Percolate. Percolator. (Of coffee.)

perfect Sheer, utter.

perform Make a fuss.

perisher Person (often **little perisher** Child) who is mildly troublesome or blameworthy.

perishing
1. Troublesome.
2. Very cold.

perk Same as **perc**.

perk up Revive.

perks Perquisites. Additional advantages or gains (usu. financial) acquired in course of one's employment, etc.

perm Permanent wave. Also [v.].

pesky Tiresome.

pet
1. [v.] Fondle amorously.
2. Intimate term of address.

Pete's sake, for Excl.

petting
1. Caressing.
2. **petting-party** One arranged for purpose of caressing.
3. **heavy petting** Specially intimate (or prolonged) caressing.

pew Seat.
- *Take a pew.*

pezazz Same as **bezazz**.

phiz(og) Face.

phoney
1. [adj.] Unreal. Not genuine. Fraudulent.
2. [n.] Person who is not what he pretends to be. Phoney thing.

phooey Nonsense.

phreak One who practises techniques of making telephone calls without payment. Usu. **phone phreak**.

phut, go Cease to function.

physical jerks Physical training exercises.

pi
1. Pious.
2. **pi-jaw** [n.] Moral lecture. Also [v.] Lecture sanctimoniously.

pickle
1. Difficult situation. Plight.
2. Urination.

pickled Intoxicated.

picky Fastidious.

picnic, no A difficult undertaking.

picture, get the Understand.

picture, in the Informed.

piddle Urinate. Also [n.].

piddling [adj.] Trifling.

pie-eyed Drunk.

pie in the sky Promise of future benefits with no guarantee or precise indication of when they will materialise.

piece Girl.

piece of cake Very easy undertaking.

piece of piss* Same as **piece of cake**.

piece of work Person (usu. derog., often **nasty piece of work**).

piece, say one's Speak one's point of view.

piffle Nonsense.

pig
1. Policeman.
2. Unpleasant person.
3. **pig in** Eat.
4. **pig it** Live in dirty or disorderly conditions.
5. Armoured car. (Military.)
6. **pig ignorant** Very ignorant.

pig's breakfast Mess. Muddle.

pig's ear, make a Blunder. Make a mess.

pigs in clover Vulgarians living in ostentatious comfort.

pigeon
1. Responsibility. Business.
2. **pigeon-livered** Cowardly.

piggy-back Child's ride on adult's back.

pile Large amount of money.

pile it on Same as **pile on the agony**.

pile, make one's Make one's fortune.

pile on the agony Exaggerate. Dramatise.

pile up [v.] Crash (usu. car).

pile-up [n.] Road accident involving car or, more usu., several cars.

pill
1. Ball.
2. Objectionable person.
3. **pills** Testicles.
4. [Abbr.] Birth-control pill. Also **on the pill** Regularly using birth-control pills.

pillock Foolish person.

pillocks Nonsense. [adj.] **pillocky**.

pillow-talk Conversation between people in bed together.

pimple Hill.

pin-head Fool. Also **pin-headed**.

pin one's hear back Listen intently.

pins Legs.

pin-up
1. Admired person.
2. Picture of favourite film-star, etc.

pinch
1. Steal.
2. Arrest.

pink
1. Mildly left-wing. Also **pinky** [n.] & [adj.]. See **pinko**.
2. **tickled pink** Vastly amused.

pink fit, have a Become very annoyed.

pink, in the
1. Fit and well.
2. See **strike me pink**.

pinko Person of left-wing attitudes. Also [adj.].

pinny Pinafore.

pint-sized Diminutive.

pip
1. [v.] Fail (e.g. an exam).
2. [v.] Defeat (e.g. in a race).
3. **give the pip** Irritate. Annoy.
4. **have the pip** Be depressed.

pipe down Be quiet.

pipe one's *or* **an eye** Weep.

pipe-opener Preliminary or mild physical exercise.

pipe up Speak (gen. unexpectedly).

pipped at the post Narrowly beaten.

pipsqueak Nondescript and insignificant person.

piss*
    1. [v.] Urinate. Also [n.] **have** *or* **do a piss**.
    2. Excl.
    3. Beer of poor quality.
    4. **go on the piss** Undertake a bout of heavy drinking.

piss about* [v.] Behave feebly and to no good purpose. Also **piss-arse about.***

piss and wind* Mere talk. Boasting.
    • *He's all piss and wind.* He talks emptily, and too much.

piss-house* Lavatory.

piss off* Depart.

piss oneself* Laugh heartily.

piss-pot* Chamber pot.

piss (out of), take the* Make fun (of). [adj. & n.] **piss-taking**.

piss-poor* Very poor.

piss-up* [n.] Bout of heavy drinking. See **organise a piss-up**.

pissed*
    1. Drunk. Also numerous expressions, e.g. **pissed as a newt, pissed up to the eyebrows** Very drunk.
    2. **pissed on from a great height** Severely reprimanded.

pisser*
    1. Penis.
    2. Objectionable fellow.
    3. Lavatory.

pit Bed.

pitch in Begin. Interfere.

pitch into Attack (verbally or physically).

pitch it hot *or* **strong** Exaggerate.

pizazz Same as **bezazz**.

places, go Be successful.

plague
1. [v.] Harass. Trouble.
2. [n.] Nuisance.

plank down Put down (esp. deposit money).

plant
1. Conceal (usu. as part of a plot).
2. Person or thing concealed thus.

plaster Bombard heavily.

plastered Drunk.

plastic Artificial. Not genuine. Similar to **phoney**.

plastic money Credit card.

plate, have enough *or* **too much** (etc.) **on one's** Have enough, too much, etc. work to do.

plate, on a In an easy form. Easily.

plate, on one's To occupy one. As one's responsibility.
• *He has a good deal of work on his plate.*

plates (of meat) Feet. [RS]

platinum blond(e) Woman with very pale golden hair (usu. bleached).

play Same as **play ball**.

play a hunch Act according to an idea, guess, suspicion.

play along with Cooperate. Agree with.

play artful Conceal one's real motives or feelings.

play ball Cooperate.

play-boy [n.] Well-to-do idler or sensualist.

play down to Lower one's standards to assumed level of one's audience.

play for time Avoid committing oneself and so gain time.

play hard to get Encourage advances by simulating reluctance.

play hell Create an uproar, fuss, etc. (and in numerous similar contexts, e.g.
- *Rich food always plays hell with my digestion*).

play hookey Play truant.

play merry hell Create a disturbance.

Play Old Harry Same as **play the devil**.

play oneself in Spend time accustoming oneself (e.g. to a new job).

play possum Pretend (usu. to be asleep, ill, or unconscious).

play silly buggers* Behave foolishly or obstructively.

play something (*or* **one's cards) close to one's chest** Act circumspectly or secretively in something.

play the devil Create discomfort or uproar. Disorganise. Render unworkable.

play up
1. Be troublesome.
2. Tease.

play up to Support. Flatter.

play with oneself Masturbate.

plebs The common people. Occ. **pleb** One of these.

plonk
1. [n.] Cheap wine.
2. [v.] Place. Usu. **plonk down** Set down (usu. firmly).

plonking Tactless. Exaggerated.

plough Fail an examination.

pluck someone's goose Humiliate someone.

plug
1. [v.] Punch. Shoot.
2. [v.] Persist doggedly. Also **plug away** *or* **along**.
3. [v.] Publicise (usu. by incessant repetition).
4. [n.] Advertisement.

plug on, pull the finish with. Cause to disappear.

plum
1. [adj.] Very desirable.
   - *A plum job.*
2. [n.] Something very desirable.

plumb Very. Completely.

plunder Gain. Profit.

plunge
1. [n.] Gamble. (Esp. **take the plunge** Take a risk.)
2. [v.] Gamble recklessly.

plush Luxurious.

po Chamber pot.

po-faced Expressionless.

pod, in Pregnant.

podge Fat person.

podgy Short and stout.

pointer Hint.

poison [n.] Drink.
   - *What's your poison?* What would you like to drink?

poison, like Very much.

poke [n.]
1. Blow with the fist. Also [v.].
2. Act of sexual intercourse. Also [v.].

pole See **up the pole**.

polish off
1. Defeat. Overwhelm.
2. Kill.

pom
1. Pomeranian dog.
2. [Abbr.] **pommy**.

pommy
1. Immigrant from England. Australian term for Englishman.
2. [adj.] English.

Pompey Portsmouth.

ponce
1. Man living off prostitute's earnings. Also [v.].
2. Objectionable man.
3. Flashily dressed ladies' man.
4. [v.] Sponge.
5. **ponce about** Flounce ostentatiously.
6. **ponce oneself up** Smarten one's appearance.
7. [adj.] **ponced up** Flashily dressed. (Often facet.) Also **poncy**.

pong Unpleasant smell. Also [v.].

pongo Soldier.

pongy Unpleasantly smelling.

ponies Racehorses.

pony £25.

pooch Small dog.

poodle-faking Devoting time to feminine society.

poof Male homosexual. [derog.] Also **poofter, pouffe, poove, puff, pouve, pouf,** etc.

pooh
1. Unpleasant smell.
2. Excl. when experiencing one.

Pool, the Liverpool.

poop Same as **peep**.

pooped Exhausted.

poor man's . . . , the A cheap equivalent of . . .

poor view of, take a Object to.

poove Same as **poof**.

pop
1. [adj.] Popular. (In numerous expressions, e.g. **pop-art, pop-culture,** to indicate up-to-date, trendy ephemera, often associated with commercial pressures.)
2. [n.] Popular music, often commercially produced for the young. Hence **pop-star, pop-concert, pop-fan**.
3. [n.] Soft drink, often fizzy.

4. [n.] Father.

5. [v.] Pawn. Also **in pop** Pawned. **pop-shop** Pawn-broker's shop.

6. Term of address to elderly man.

pop-eyed With eyes bulging (usu. from astonishment).

pop off
1. Depart quickly.
2. Die.

pop the question Propose marriage.

popper Press-stud.

poppet
1. Attractive woman or child. Kind woman.
2. Term of endearment or approbation.

poppycock Nonsense.

popsy Young woman. Also **popsie**.

porky Fat.

porn(o) Pornography; pornographic. Hence **porn-shop, porn-film, porn-show,** etc.

porpoise Fat person.

porridge Prison, or a prison-sentence. Usu. **do porridge** Serve a term in prison.

posh
1. Smart. Superior.
2. **posh up** Make smart.

positive Downright.
   • *A positive nuisance.*

posted, keep one Keep one informed and up-to-date with news.

poss Possible.

pot
1. Large sum of money. Also **pots of money** Large quantities of money.
2. Trophy. **pot-hunter** One excessively devoted to winning competitions, prizes, etc.
3. Person (as in **fuss-pot,** etc.).

4. Paunch. **pot-bellied** Having prominent paunch.
5. Marijuana. Also **pot-head** Person who smokes marijuana.
6. [v.] Put child on chamber pot.
7. **piss-pot*** Chamber pot.

pot, all to Confused. Bungled.

pot, go to Fall into poor condition.

potato
1. Hole in stockings.
2. See **hot potato**.

pots of A lot of.

potty
1. [adj.] Crazy.
2. Insignificant.
3. [n.] Chamber pot.

pouf See **poof**.

pound-not(e)ish Affectedly aristocratic.

pow Impact of personality.

pow-wow Consultation. Discussion.

powder one's jacket Thrash one.

powder one's nose Go to the lavatory. (Women only.)

power of, a A great deal of.

pox Syphilis.

pozzy Jam.

prang [n.] & [v.] Crash.

prat Foolish person. Also **prat-face**.

prawn Fool.

preachify Deliver a long and boring sermon.

preachy prone to preaching.

precious
1. Very (e.g. **precious little, precious few,** etc.).
2. Meaningless adj. expressing irritation.
   • *I'm tired of him and his precious troubles.*
3. Notable. [derog.] Very bad. Considerable.

prefab
1. Prefabricated.
2. Prefabricated building.

prelim Preliminary examination.

prelims Pages of book before main text (e.g. title-page, preface, contents list, etc.).

prep
1. Homework.
2. **prep school** Preparatory school.

press on regardless Continue to work.

press the button Begin. Take initial action.

Preston Guild, every Very rarely.

pretty Fairly. Rather. See **sit pretty**.

pretty as paint Very pretty.

pretty well Almost completely.

previous Early. Hasty.

priceless
1. Extremely funny.
2. (Of people) Notable.
   - *A priceless idiot.*

pricey Expensive.

prick*
1. Penis.
2. Abusive or contemptuous term (applied to men).
3. **prick-teaser**. See **cock-teaser**.

print, the The printing trade.

private eye Private detective.

prize Conspicuous. Egregious.
- *A prize nit-wit.*

pro
1. [adj.] & [n.] Professional.
2. [n.] Prostitute.
3. **pro tem** For the time being.

prof Professor.

proles, the The mindless masses.

prom
1. Promenade.
2. Promenade concert.

pronto Promptly.

prop Propeller. Stage property.

proper
1. Real. Genuine. Excellent. Thorough.
2. Extremely.

proposition
1. Problem. Task. Prospect. Opponent.
2. [v.] Make proposal (esp. invitation of sexual nature).

props
1. Small portable articles necessary in staging a play.
2. The person who looks after these.

pros Proscenium.

proud, do (person) Behave generally or in creditable way to (person).

prune Foolish, ineffectual person.

pseud Pretentious or affected person, usu. in literary circles. Also [adj.].

psyche [v.]
1. Affect mentally. Influence motivation by 'psychological' tactics.
2. **psyche up** Boost morale in.
3. **psyche out** Demoralise.
4. **psyching** Doing thus.

psycho Mentally deranged (person).

psychological moment Appropriate or crucial time.

pub Public house.

pub-crawl Tour of public houses for bout of drinking.

pud Pudding.

pudden(-head)
  1. Term of facet. mild abuse.
  2. Foolish person.

pudding Uninteresting, dull person.

pudding (*or* **pudden**) **club, in the** Pregnant.

puddled Confused. Half-witted.

puff
  1. Same as **poof**.
  2. Breath. **out of puff** Breathless, puffed.

puff-puff Train. [Juv.] Also **puffer**.

puffter Same as **poof**.

puffy Effeminate. Affected. (From **puff**.)

pug-ugly Very ugly.

pukka Genuine. Of good quality.

pukka sahib Perfect gentleman. (Now usu. facet.)

pull Do. Commit. Perform. Attract. Attempt.

pull a fast one Take advantage. Trick. Deceive. Evade.

pull (all) the stops out Make every effort.

pull in
  1. Arrest.
  2. Earn.

pull off
  1. Win.
  2. Bring to a successful conclusion.
  3. Masturbate.

pull one's finger out See **finger out**.

pull one's leg Tease one.

pull one's socks up Make a better effort.

pull-through Very thin man.

pump ship Urinate.

punch Energy. Drive. Vigour. Force. Attack.

punch-line Most important (usu. final) part of joke (or speech, statement etc.).

punch-up [n.] Fight.

punch up the bracket Punch on the nose.

punk
1. [n.] Nonsense.
2. [adj.] Worthless. Loutish.
3. [n.] Detestable person. Lout.
4. Style of music, dress or behaviour characterised by disregard of convention.

punter Customer. Client.

purler
1. Heavy fall. **come** *or* **take a purler** Fall heavily.
2. Heavy blow with fist.

purple Sensational, clumsily heightened or floridly emotional.

purple heart Amphetamine pill or capsule.

push
1. [n.]Dismissal. Esp. **get the push** Be dismissed.
2. [v.] Sell (of drugs, shares, etc.). [n.] **pusher**.

push around Harass. Nag. Treat without consideration.

push back Swallow. Gulp down.

push-bike Bicycle.

push comes to shove, when When matters become difficult. If it is necessary to make a difficult choice.

push off Go away.

push one's face in Punch one.

push the boat out
1. Start.
2. Be generous with money. Celebrate.

push (up the) daisies Be in one's grave.

pushed
1. Worried. Harassed.
2. Late. Short of time. Also **pushed for time**.
3. Extremely busy.
4. Short of cash.

pusher One who sells drugs or shares, etc.

pushing daisies Dead and buried. Also **pushing up (the) daisies**.

pushover
1. Easy matter to accomplish.
2. Easy prey. Person easy to convince or deceive.

pushy Self-assertive.

puss(y) (-cat)
1. Girl.
2. Female private parts.
3. Cat.

pussyfoot
1. [v.] Tread gently. Behave with delicacy.
2. [n.] Cautious person. (Often derog.)

put a sock in it Stop talking.

put the finger on Identify.

put a jerk in it Show more vigour or activity.

put away
1. Imprison. Confine in mental hospital.
2. Consume. Eat. Drink.

put in Spend (time).

put in a good word for Speak in favour of (usu. a person).

put in the picture Inform. Bring (person) up to date.

put inside Send to prison.

put it across one
1. Punish one.
2. Deceive one.

put it on Pretend. Show off.

put it there! Shake hands!

put-on [n.] Trick.

put on side Assume an arrogant manner.

put on the spot Place in a position of difficulty, embarrassment, etc.

put one's eye in a sling Administer a black eye. Rebuke. Rebuff. Thwart. Defeat.

put one's feet up Rest.

put one's finger on Express, discern, identify (usu. a problem) exactly.

put one's money where one's mouth is Support one's opinion by action.

put one's shirt on Wager everything on.

put one's skates on Hurry.

put one's thinking cap on Meditate on a problem.

put out to grass *or* **graze** See **grass (4)**.

put paid to End. Defeat.

put that in your pipe and smoke it! Just you consider that!

put the bite on Extort from.

put the boot in
1. Take vigorously decisive action (usu. unpleasant).
2. Kick. Attack person by kicking.

put the screws on Coerce.

put the tin *or* **top hat** *or* **the (tin) lid on** Finish. Create a severe set-back. Bring to the limit of endurance.

put the wind up Frighten.

put-up job Deliberately planned happening (usu. with deceitful or criminal intent).

put years on one [Lit.] Shorten one's life. [Met.] Weary. Bore, irritate, annoy, etc., intensely.

put wise to Make conversant with.

putrid Extremely bad.

pyjamas, the cat's Exactly what's wanted.

Q

QT, on the (strict) Surreptitiously.

quack Doctor.

quad Quadrangle. See also **quod**.

quads Quadruplets.

quarrel with one's bread and butter Behave so as to endanger one's livelihood.

quean Homosexual male, esp. one with flamboyantly effeminate mannerisms. Often **queen**.

queen Elderly, passive homosexual male [Adj.] **queeny** See **quean**.

Queen Bee Senior woman in an organisation. Dominant woman.

queer
   1. [n.] Homosexual male. Also [adj.].
   2. [v.] Spoil. Put out of order.
   3. **queer bird, card, cove, customer, fish, stick,** etc. Eccentric, odd person.

queer one's pitch Spoil one's plans or chances (usu. by anticipation or imitation).

Queer Street, in In difficulties.

question, pop the Make a proposal of marriage.

quick one [n.] Drink (usu. in a hurry).

quickie Brief matter, short question, or any other brief performance.

quid £1. Also **half a quid** 50p.

quid deal A pound's worth, or any quantity, of drugs.

quids in Enjoying fortunate success.

quim* Female private parts.

quins Quintuplets.

quite a bit
1. Fairly frequently or much.
2. A good amount.

quod Prison.

quote Quotation.

quotes Quotation marks.

R

rabbit
1. [n.] Inadequate performer at games or sport.
2. [v.] Grumble.
3. [v.] Talk. Usu. **rabbit** Talk incessantly.
4. **rabbit('s) punch** Disabling blow on back of neck.
5. **rabbit food** Salad, esp. lettuce.

racket
1. Criminal or shady dealings. Dodge. Scheme for making money or achieving success.
2. Business, profession, etc.
3. **stand the racket** Take the responsibility. Pay the bill.

rag
1. **lose one's rag** Same as **get one's rag out**.
2. [n.] Undergraduate jollification for charitable purposes. Prank.
3. [v.] Play practical jokes. Create joyful uproar.
4. **chew the rag** Grumble. Complain. Argue. Discuss.
5. [n.] Newspaper.

rag-bag Mess. Collection of miscellaneous objects.

rag-trade Tailoring and dressmaking.

ragged-arse(d)* [adj.] Disreputable. Tattered.

rain stair-rods Rain in a straight, heavy, vertical downpour.

raise Find, or be able to speak to, person wanted.

raise a stink Create a scandal.

raise Cain Cause a disturbance. Make an angry scene.

raise hell Create uproar, fuss, disturbance, etc.

rake it in
1. Earn much money quickly.
2. **rake in** (of money) Earn, gain, receive as takings.

rake-off [n.] Commission. Profit.

ram-jam full Crammed full.

ramp [n.] Swindle.

rap Punishment. Blame.

rap, take the Take responsibility or punishment (usu. for someone else's fault).

raspberry
1. Sound imitating breaking of wind, and expressing derision or disapproval.
2. **get** *or* **give the raspberry** Receive *or* express disapproval.

rat [n.] Gen. term of contempt.

rat (on) [v.] Betray. Inform to the police or other authority. Go back on (one's word).

rat-bag Very unpleasant or worthless person.

rat-race, the Society, or the business of living in a society, where competitiveness and ruthless competition are necessary or believed to be so.

rat-trap Mouth.

rate Esteem highly.

rate of knots, at a (great) Very quickly.

rather! Excl. of disbelief.

rats! Excl. of disbelief.

rattle along Move quickly.

rattled Confused. Nonplussed. Angry. Frightened. Flustered.

ratty Annoyed. Irritable. Irritated.

rave
1. A party (usu. wild). [Pop.] Often **rave-up** Specially hectic social occasion. Also **raver** Wild youth [Pop.]. Sexually promiscuous woman.

2. **rave notice** Extremely enthusiastic press-review of play, etc.

raw, in the Naked.

razz(a)mataz(z) Jazz. Flashy display. Coarsely loud and excitingly colourful exhibition, event, behaviour, etc.

razzle Excitement. Bustle. Spree.

razzle, on the On a spree, often drunken.

razzle-dazzle Spree.

reach-me-down Second-hand clothes. Cheap clothes.

read the riot act Scold at length.

ready, the [n.] Available cash.

real, for [n.] Genuine.

real live Emph. (usu. facet) adj. phrase adding nothing to the actual meaning of the noun.

real McCoy, the That which is absolutely genuine.

rebound, on the After refusal by another.

recap Recapitulate. Recapitulation.

recce Reconnaissance. Reconnoitre.

record, change the Stop repeating the same thing incessantly.

red Left-wing politically. Also [n.].

red biddy Cheap red wine.

red duster Red Ensign.

red-hot Extreme. Enthusiastic. Valuable. Knowledgeable. Keen.

red lamp (light) district One given over to brothels.

red neck Roman Catholic.

red, see Become angry.

red! was my (etc.) **face** I (etc.) was ashamed, embarrassed.

reefer Drugged cigarette (usu. marijuana).

ref [n.] and [v.] Referee.

refresher Drink.

regardless See **press on**.

regular
1. Genuine; real.
2. Not constipated.

regulars Regular customers, patrons, etc.

rent boy Young male prostitute.

rep
1. Repertory company.
2. Representative (of business, etc.).

resting Unemployed (Theat. euphemism).

retreat into one's shell Become taciturn.

rev
1. Term of address to minister of religion.
2. Revolution of an engine. Also [v.] Cause engine to revolve.

reviver Drink.

rhino
1. Money.
2. Rhinoceros.

rib [v.] Tease.

rib-tickling [adj.] Amusing.

rich Preposterous. Absurd.

ride [n.] Sexual intercourse. Also [v.].

ride, take for a Deceive. Mislead.

rig [n.] Style for dress. Also **rig-out** Outfit. **rig out** [v.] Dress.

right Extreme. E.g. **right bastard** Very unpleasant man.

right away Immediately.

right, bit of all Person or thing approved of.

right Charlie See **Charlie**.

right-down Utter.

right foot foremost See **best foot**.

right-(h)o (*or* **-oh**) I agree. Also **righto, righti(-)o, righty-o(h)** *or* **-ho**, etc.

right in the head Sane.

right on Absolutely correct. I agree.

right there, put it Shake hands.

right wing, the Those of politically Conservative persuasion. Also [adj.].

right you are I agree.

rigid, bore Bore severely.

rile [v.] Anger. Annoy.

Riley/Reilly, the life of A very enjoyable existence.

ring
  1. [n.] Female private parts.
  2. [v.] Change (usu. shadily). Cheat.

ring a bell Bring something to one's mind.

ring, give a [v.] Telephone.

ring the changes Attempt to various alternatives successively.

rinse one's teeth *or* **gums** Have a drink.

riot Amusing person or thing.

rip off [v.] Filch. Steal. Defraud. Rob.

rip-off [n.] Fraud. Theft. Piece of exorbitant profiteering.

rip-snorter Anything specially pleasing, esp. wildly adventurous story. [adj.] **rip-snorting**.

ripping Excellent. (Old f., therefore facet.)

rise and shine Get out of bed.

ritzy Wealthy, superior, fashionable, stylish.

river, sell down the Betray.

road
  1. Way.
     • *He keeps getting in my road.*
  2. **any road** Anyway.

road show Travelling entertainment.

roast
1. [v.] Scold.
2. **get** *or* **give a roasting** Receive *or* deliver a reprimand.

robbed Cheated. Swindled. Often **we was robbed** (in sport) We were extremely unlucky. The referee was against us.

rock
1. [n.] Jewel (usu. plural).
2. [v.] Startle (usu. with news).

rock the boat Render things difficult for one's colleagues.

rocker Member of teenage gang addicted to motor-cycles and distinctive life-style.

rocker, off one's Crazy.

rocket Severe reprimand. Also [v.] Chastise severely.

rocks, on the
1. With ice (usu. of drinks, esp. Scotch).
2. Penniless.

rocky Unsteady.

roger [v.]
1. Have sexual intercourse with. Also [n.] **rogering**.
2. Scold.
3. I agree.

roll [v.] Physically assault (usu. to rob). Also [n.] Sexual intercourse.

roll back Reverse a trend in.
• *Roll back prices to their level of last year.*

roll in the aisles
1. Laugh heartily in a theatre, etc.
2. Cause an audience to laugh thus.

roll on . . . May . . . soon arrive or happen.

roll-on Feminine undergarment.

roll-on, roll-off [adj.] Capable of being driven on to and off. (Of boat, aircraft, train, etc., capable of carrying vehicles which are driven on and off by the drivers themselves.)

roll up Assemble. Arrive.

Roller Same as **Rolls**.

rollick [v.] Scold severely. Also **rollock**.

rollicking Severe scolding. Also **rollocking**.

rolling (in it) Very wealthy.

rollocks Polite evasion of **bollocks**. See also **rollick**.

Rolls Rolls-Royce car.

romp Move quickly and without effort.

romp away with Win (something, usu. a race) easily. Also **romp home**.

roof, hit *or* **go through the** Become very angry.

rook [v.] & [n.] Cheat.

rookie New recruit. Also **rook(e)y**.

roomer Lodger.

root about [n.] & [v.] Search.

root for Support (usu. vociferously).

rop(e)y Unsatisfactory. Untidily organised. Decrepit. Inefficient. Badly arranged.

rorty First-class. Spirited.

Rosie *or* **-y Lee** Tea.

rot Nonsense. Also excl.

rot about [v.] Idle.

rot-gut Powerful or disagreeable alcoholic drink. (Also facet.)

rotten Disagreeable. Regrettable. Ill-advised (of state of affairs only). Unwell.

rotter Offensive person.

rough
   1. Unfairly harsh.
   2. See also **cut up**.
   3. Unwell.
   4. [Abbr.] **rough neck**.

rough house Brawl. Disorder.

rough neck Lout.

rough on Severe or unfortunate for.

rough stuff Rough behaviour.

rough up Assault.

round in circles, run *or* **go** Be active, often without result.

round the bent *or* **twist** Mad. Also **clean round the bend**.

rounds of the kitchen, give one the Scold one.

row
1. [n.] Noise. Quarrel. Commotion.
2. [v.] Make noise or commotion. Also **make a row**.
3. [v.] Quarrel. Also **have a row**.
4. **kick up a row** Make a protest.

row of beans, another Quite another matter.

rozzer Policeman.

rub in Over-emphasise; repeat naggingly and irritatingly.
- *I did wrong but I wish he wouldn't keep rubbing it in.*

rub out Kill.

rub up Caress intimately for sexual excitement. [n.] **rub-up**.

rub up the wrong way Antagonise.

rubber Condom.

rubber-neck Persistently inquisitive person. Habitual sightseer. Excessively familiar person. Also [v.] Behave as such.

rubbish [v.] Express scorn or contempt for.

ruction(s) Uproar. Quarrel.

ruddy Polite evasion of **bloody**.

rugger Rugby football.

rum [adj.] Queer. Odd.

rum customer Person difficult to fathom or deal with.

rum do *or* **go** Puzzling or mysterious event.

rum one Odd person. Puzzling affair.

rum 'un Same as **rum one**.

rumble
1. [v.] Discover motives or nature (of a person). Detect. Comprehend. Guess. Catch out.
2. [n.] Gang fight.

rummy Same as **rum**.

rumpus Disturbance. Brawl. Row. Uproar.

run-about Car, usu. small, not intended for long journeys or major use.

run-around, give one (*or* get) the Treat one (*or* be treated) casually or contemptuously, causing one to be inconvenienced for no good reason.

run away and play trains Facet. term of dismissal.

run in Arrest.

run off one's legs *or* feet, be Be exceedingly busy.

run one's head into a brick wall *or* a post
1. Behave obstinately. Persevere stupidly.
2. Encounter insuperable difficulties.

run out on Leave in the lurch.

run the show Manage an enterprise.

run the tape over Examine (usu. medically).

runner Vehicle in running order.

running jump at oneself, take a Expression indicating refusal. Usu. **go and take a . . .** etc.

runs, the Diarrhoea.

rush [v.]
1. Charge (often excessively).
2. Cost.

rush-job Task that has to be finished quickly.

rush of brains to the head Bright idea. Usu. facet. or derog.

Ruskies Russians.

rustle up Provide. Find.

S

sack
1. Dismiss from employment. Also **give the sack**.
2. **get the sack** Be dismissed from employment.
3. Bed.

sahib See **pukka**.

sail in(to)
1. Make a vigorous beginning to.
2. Enter.
3. Attack physically.

sailor's friend Moon.

salt
1. [n.] Sailor (usu. **old salt**).
2. [v.] Save (money). Usu. **salt away** Put (money) into safe keeping.

salts, like a dose of Very rapidly.

sambo* Negro. [Derog.]

same here The same applies to me.

same street, not in the Not in the same class, category. Of a different (usu. poorer) quality.

same to you with knobs on Facet. meaningless retort expressing rejection of what has just been said.

samey Monotonously unrelieved.

san Sanatorium.

sap [n.] Simpleton.

sarge Sergeant.

sarky Sarcastic.

sarny Sandwich.

sat (up)on Suppressed.

sauce Impertinence. Also [v.] Show impertinence.

sauce-box Impertinent person.

saucy (Of film, play, etc.) Mildly indecent or suggestive.

sausage
1. Affectionate term of address.
2. **not a sausage** Not a thing. No money.

sausage dog Dachshund.

saved by the bell Luckily enabled to avoid difficulty.

savvy
1. [n.] Common sense.
2. [v.] Understood. Understand.

saw-bones Surgeon.

saw you coming Realised your ignorance or innocence.

say it with flowers Convey a message with a gift of flowers. Convey a message pleasantly and politely.

say goodnight to Write off. Regard as lost.

say knife, before one can Very quickly.

say-so Permission. Authority.

say when Request for advice as to how much drink (usu. alcoholic) one wants pouring.

scab Person who works when others (usu. his colleagues) are on strike. Also [adj.] and [v.].

scallywag Disreputable person. Rascal. (usu. facet.)

scanties Flimsy female underwear.

scarce, make oneself Keep out of the way.

scare the pants off Terrify.

scared stiff Terrified.

scarper Run away. Escape.

scat Depart hurriedly.

scatty Crazy. Confused. (Of people.)

scene Characteristic mode of living. Taste. Area of one's personal interests or abilities. Events, fashions or beliefs, or the places where they are to be found. [Pop.] **it's not my scene** It is not to my taste. It is not the sort of thing I know much about or understand.

schmaltz
1. Sentimental content in play, music, etc.
2. [adj.] **schmaltzy**.

schmuck Fool.

schnorrer Beggar.

schol Scholarship.

schols Scholarship examination(s).

scoff
1. [n.] Food.
2. [v.] Eat (greedily).

scoop
1. [n.] Important news obtained and published before it is known to rival newspapers. Similar advantage in business, commerce, etc.
2. [v.] Succeed in obtaining such news. Succeed in making large profit quickly or by anticipating competitors.

scoot Depart (hurriedly). Go (quickly).

scorch Travel very rapidly (usu. by car).

scorcher
1. Hot day.
2. Person or thing attracting great admiration.

score
1. Situation. News. Esp. **what's the score?** What's happening?
2. [v.] Obtain drugs illegally.
3. Find (sexual) favour with a person.

score off Achieve success against (a person, usu. to his detriment).

score points off Achieve success against (person) in argument.

Scotch mist
1. Rain.
2. Used sarcastically in numerous contexts when the person addressed appears to be unobservant. Thus a person searching for something which is under his nose will be told
- *There it is, unless it's Scotch mist.*

Scotty Scotsman.

scouse
1. Stew.
2. Abbr. of **scouser**.

scouser Person from Liverpool.

scrag Manhandle roughly (person).

scram Depart.

scrambled egg Gold decoration on cap of senior officer.

scrap [n.] & [v.] Fight (usu. with the fists).

scrape
1. [n.] & [v.] Shave.
2. Cheap butter, or a thin layer of butter.
3. **scrape the (bottom of the) barrel** Use the last remnants of one's resources to accomplish something.

scratch along Manage to live.

scream [n.] Hilarious person or thing.

screamer Fine example.

screaming (h)abdabs, give one the Make one intensely irritable or annoyed.

screw
1. [n.] Prison warder.
2. [n.] Wages; salary.
3. [n.] Sexual intercourse. Woman viewed as partner in this.*
4. [v.] Copulate with (woman).*
5. **put the screws on** Apply pressure to.

screw loose, have a Be slightly mad.

screwball Eccentric person.

screwed on (the right way), have one's head Be sensible, shrewd.

screwed up
1. Angry.
2. Neurotic.

screw up Bungle.

screwy Eccentric. Mad.

scrimshank [v.] Shirk duty.

scrimshanker Shirker.

scrounge
1. [v.] Cadge. Steal. Search for.
2. **scrounger** One who does this.
3. **be on the scrounge** Beg.

scrub
1. Cheap prostitute.
2. Cancel.
3. **scrub it!** Forget it.
4. **scrub round** Ignore. Cancel.

scrubber Slovenly girl. Cheap prostitute.

scruff Untidy or uncouth person. [adj.] **scruffy**.

scrum Tightly pressed crowd.

scrump Steal apples.

scrumptious Extremely delightful.

scuffer Policeman.

sculling around
1. (Of things) Scattered about; left lying about unused.
2. (Of people) Wandering aimlessly.

scupper [v.] Put an end to (plan, etc.). Defeat. Ruin.

sea-lawyer Same as **barrack-room lawyer**.

search me! I don't know!

seat of one's pants, by the Instinctively.

sec Second.

see a man about a dog, go to Go to the lavatory.

226

see how the land lies Discover what the position is.

see off Defeat. Outwit. Finish.

see one damned (*or* **in hell** *or* **hanged**) **first** Refuse emphatically to accept one's proposals, etc.

see red Become angry.

see you! Good bye!

seedy Shabby. Feeling ill.

sell out [v.] Betray.

sell-out [n.] Betrayal.

semi Semi-detached house.

send Transport with rapture. Also **get sent** Be affected thus.

send up [v.] Make fun of (usu. by parody).

send-up [n.] Parody.

sent Transported with rapture.

serve out Take revenge on.

service See **get some service in**.

set about Attack.

set back Cost.

set up [v.] Devise plot to betray.

set-up [n.] The general arrangement of an organisation.

set oneself up as Pretend to be.

settle for Finally decide to accept.

settle one's hash Subdue. Defeat. Kill. Get the better of one.

sew up Organise. Arrange. Settle. Complete.

sex-kitten (*or* **-pot**) Young woman conscious of her charms and anxious that they should be appreciated by men.

sez you! Excl. of mild derision.

shack up Live. Cohabit.

shack up with Live with (esp. though unmarried).

shaft* [v.] Copulate with.

shag*
1. [v.] Copulate with.
2. [n.] Copulation. Person viewed as partner in this.

shagged (out) Exhausted.

shake
1. [v.] Shake hands. Esp. **shake on it** Conclude a deal by shaking hands.
2. **shake down** Become comfortably settled.

shake a leg Hurry. Make a start. Dance.

shake-out Reorganisation (of factory, etc.) usu. involving dismissal of personnel.

shake-up Reorganisation. (E.g.
- *Cabinet shake-up.* A change of personnel.)

shakes Condition of trembling brought on by illness, drinking, apprehension, etc.

shakes, no great Not very good or efficient.

shamateur Person claiming to be amateur (esp. in sport) but in fact receiving indirect payment.

shambles Confusion. Mess. Muddle.

shanghai [v.] Kidnap. Trick.

sharp
1. [adj.] Smart, or over-smart, in dress.
2. **be** *or* **look sharp** Hurry.

sharp end, the (Of activity, organisation etc.) The most difficult or crucial aspect.

sharpish Fairly or very quickly.

shat* See **shit on**.

shattered Exhausted. Overwhelmed.

shattering Very upsetting or striking.

shaver Fellow. Usu. **young shaver** Mischievous boy.

she-dragon Forbidding woman.

shebang, the whole The entire matter, business, thing, etc.

sheets in the wind, three Drunk.

sheila Young woman.

shekels Money.

shell-like [n.] Ear.

shell out Pay.

shelling peas, easy as Very easy.

shemozzle
1. Uproar. Commotion. Dispute.
2. Same as **shebang**.

shenannicking, shenanigan Trickery. (Several other spellings exist.)

shift [v.] Move rapidly. Consume large quantities (usu. of food or drink).

shindig Uproar. Fuss. Party.

shine off, take the Reduce the enjoyment or value of.

shine to *or* **for, take a** Take a fancy for.

shiner Black eye.

shirt See **lay one's shirt**.

shirt on, keep one's Keep calm.

shirt on, put one's Wager everything one has.

shirty Annoyed. Ill-tempered.

shit*
1. [n.] Ordure. Defecation.
2. [n.] Term of address of extreme abuse. Also **shit-house, shit-bag**.
3. Generally applied to anything objectionable or unacceptable; also in numerous expressions, e.g. **in the shit** In trouble; **in shit order** In extreme disorder; **shit-stirrer** Trouble-maker; **shit bricks** Be apprehensive. Defecate with difficulty; **shit-scared** Very frightened.
4. [v.] Defecate.
5. Excl. of displeasure. Also **shit a brick! shit and derision!** etc.
6. Abbr. of **bull-shit**.
7. Hashish.

shit on*
1. [v.] Reprimand. Usu. **shat on (from a great** *or* **dizzy height)** Reprimanded (very severely). Placed in serious difficulty.
2. **shit on one's own doorstep** Make trouble for oneself.

shit-hot* Very enthusiastic, efficient.

shit-house*
1. Lavatory.
2. Term of address, extremely abusive.

shite* [n.] & [v.] Variant of **shit**.

shocker Disagreeable, displeasing or inefficient person or thing.

shoe-string [adj.] With very little money at disposal.

shoe-string, on a Cheaply.

shook Surprised severely.
- *That shook him!*

shook up Upset.

shoot
1. Speak out.
2. **shoot the lights** Pass traffic lights when one ought not to, esp. when they show amber.

shoot a line
1. Boast. [n.] **line-shooter** Boaster.
2. Talk too much.

shoot down (in flames) Defeat (usu. in argument).

shoot oneself in the foot Make a mistake that damages oneself.

shoot one's mouth off
1. Boast.
2. Talk indiscreetly.

shoot, the whole (bang) The entire amount, affair, business, thing, etc.

shoot up Inject (narcotics etc.).

shooter Gun. Also **shooting-iron**.

shooting-match, the whole Same as **the whole shoot** (under **shoot, the whole**).

shoot-out Gun-battle.

shop
1. [v.] Get someone into trouble. Betray. Inform against.
2. [n.] Place of work.
3. **talk shop** Discuss one's occupation.
4. **all over the shop** In disorder. In every direction.
5. **come to the wrong shop** Apply to the wrong person.

short
1. [n.] Short film.
2. [n.] & [v.] Short circuit.
3. Drink of spirits as distinct from drink (e.g. beer) taken in larger quantity. Also **something short**.
4. See **caught short, taken short**.

short and curlies, have by the Have at one's mercy.

short-arse*
1. A short person.
2. [adj.] **short-arsed** Small. (Of person.)

short hairs, have one by the Have control over one. Have one at a disadvantage.

short on Lacking in.

shot
1. Dram (of spirits).
2. Dose (of drug).
3. **have a shot at** Attempt.
4. **shot at** [adj.] Exhausted.

shot at dawn, be Be in serious trouble.

shot down See **shoot down**.

shot of, be *or* **get** Be *or* get rid of.

shout
1. [n.] Turn to pay a round of drinks. Also [v.] Pay for drinks.
2. **shout the odds** Talk too much. Boast. Proclaim one's views loudly.

shove
1. Depart. Also **shove along** *or* **off**.
2. Put.
   - *Shove it in the drawer.*

shove, the Dismissal.

show
1. [n.] Any form of public entertainment. **do a show** Visit a theatre, cinema, etc. **show-stopper** Performance that is much applauded.
2. [n.] Concern. Undertaking. Organisation. Hence **run** *or* **boss the show** Assume control.
3. **give the show away** Reveal the truth.
4. **put up a good** (etc.) **show** Give a good (etc.) account of oneself.
5. **steal the show** Be more successful than anyone else present (usu. by excellent performance in public, e.g. in play.)
6. **a poor show** A regrettable occurrence.
7. **good show!** Good!

show biz The entertainment industry.

show-down Clash of opposing views (usu. in circumstances where resolution of clash is being sought).

show a leg Get out of bed.

show the flag Make an appearance out of a sense of duty.

show up Appear. Be present.

shower Disagreeable person or, more usu., group of people. **shower of shit*** Extremely disagreeable person(s).

shrink [n.] Psychiatrist. Psychologist. Abbr. **head-shrinker**.

shucks! Excl. of disgust or disbelief.

shufti *or* **-y** [n.] Look.

shunt Collision of vehicles.

shunt (off) Shift responsibility for something on to someone else.

shush [v.] Be quiet.

shut-eye [n.] Sleep.

shut it Same as **shut up**.

shut of, be *or* **get** Be *or* get rid of.

shut one's face *or* **mouth** *or* **trap** Stop talking.

shut up Stop talking.

shutters up, put the Become defensive or uncommunicative.

shy
1. [n.] & [v.] Throw.
2. Short (of).

shyster Tricky, dishonest person.

sick
1. Disgusted. Very upset.
2. **sick to death of** Utterly disgusted with. Tired of.
3. (Of humour) Cruel, morbid.

sick as a dog, be Vomit violently.

sick-making Sickening.

sick up [v.] Vomit.

side
1. Assumption of superiority. Often **put on side** Swagger.
2. **a bit on the side** Sexual intercourse with someone other than one's husband or wife.

side-kick Assistant. Close companion.

sideways, knock Shock deeply. Surprise considerably.

sight Great deal. Often **a darned sight more** A lot more.

sign on the dotted line Sign one's name.

silly billy Affectionate term of reproach to child who has behaved mildly foolishly.

silly buggers, play* Behave foolishly or provocatively, or both.

silly moo Term of address (to woman) See **moo**.

sin, live in Cohabit without marriage.

since Adam was a lad Since long ago.

sing Inform to police.

sink [v.] Drink.

sir [n.] One's teacher at school.

sissy Effeminate boy or man.

sister Term of address to woman.

sit-down strike Strike in which workers do not work but remain or assemble at place of work.

sit-in [n.] Form of protest by occupying premises and remaining there.

sit on Snub. Suppress. Rebuke.

sit pretty Be comfortably or advantageously placed.

sit tight Remain in one's place.

sit up and take notice Show a sudden interest.

sit-upon [n.] Posterior.

sitter An easy task.

six See **hit for six**.

sixty-four thousand dollar question, the The crucial, most important, most difficult question.

size up Form judgement of.

size of (it), the What (it) amounts to.

skate Troublesome person (usu. young).

skates on, get one's Hurry.

skedaddle Depart (usu. hurriedly).

skew-whiff Askew.

skid-lid Crash helmet.

skids on, put the Slow down.

skin [v.] Take money from extortionately.

skin alive Thrash.

skin-flick Pornographic film.

skin, get under one's Irritate one.

skin-game
  1. Swindle.
  2. Plastic surgery on the face.

skin off one's nose, no No concern of, or inconvenience to, one.

skinful, have a Drink too much alcohol.

skinhead Youth, often ruffian, with hair shaven off (as sign of membership of gang).

skinned, keep one's eyes Be wary.

skins Alternative plural of **skinhead**.

skint Without, or almost without, money.

skip [v.] Disappear. Fail to take part in.

skip it Forget about it; do not trouble.

skipper Boss.

skirt Same as **crumpet**.

skive
1. [v.] Avoid duty. Also **skive off**.
2. [v.] Evasion of duty. Undemanding task. Opportunity for idleness.

skiver Shirker.

skivvy
1. [n.] Drudge.
2. [v.] Work as drudge.

skulduggery Dishonesty.

sky-blue pink Of indeterminate colour.

sky-jack [v.] Hi-jack an aircraft. Also [n.].

sky's the limit, the There is no end to the opportunities.

slacker Lazy person.

slag
1. Unattractive but sexually alert woman.
2. Prostitute.
3. Disagreeable woman.

slag off Damn. Criticise. Ridicule.

slam Strike. Punch. Defeat heavily. Criticise.

slammer Prison.

slanging match Quarrel characterised by exchange of abuse.

slap and tickle Flirtatious behaviour.

slap down Reprove.

slap-happy Happy-go-lucky.

slap in the eye, better than a Acceptable.

slap-up Excellent. First-class. Extravagant. (Usu. of meal.)

slash
1. [n.] Urination.
2. [v.] Cut person with razor (usu. across face).

slate [v.] Criticise severely. Abuse. Scold. [n.] **slating**.

slate loose, have a Be slightly crazy.

slate, on the To be paid for later.

slave one's guts out Work excessively hard.

slay Overwhelm with surprise or amusement.

sleazy Dilapidated. (Usu. applied to cheap and gloomy places of entertainment.)

sleep around Be sexually promiscuous.

sleep, put to Painlessly kill (of animals).

sleepers Barbiturate drug.

slewed Drunk.

slide Depart.

sling
1. Throw (away). Abandon. Place (e.g.
   • *Sling it in the oven*).
2. **sling a yarn** Tell a story.
3. **sling one's hook** Depart.
4. **sling over** Pass.
5. See **mud-slinging**.

slip it across one Trick one.

slip up Make an error.

slip-up [n.] Error.

slipping Losing control, efficiency, etc.

slippy Quick. Usu. **look slippy** Be quick.

slob Disagreeable man (usu. stupid and loutish).

slog [n.] Period of intense effort.

slogger Dogged worker.

slope (off) Depart (usu. furtively).

slosh
1. [n.] Nonsense.
2. [v.] Hit hard.
3. Splash.

sloshed Drunk.

sloshy Maudlin.

slouch, no Not an incompetent person.

slug
1. [n.] Dram of spirits.
2. [v.] Hit heavily.

slurp Eat or drink noisily.

slyboots Crafty person. [Facet.]

smack
1. [n.] Heroin.
2. Exactly.

smack at, have a Make an attempt at.

smack in the eye Rebuff.

smacker
1. £1. Also **smackeroo, smackeroony**.
2. Kiss.

smack-head Heroin addict.

small-time [adj.] Unimportant. Insignificant.

smalls Underclothes.

smarm Fawn.

smarmy Insincerely polite or flattering by nature.

smart arse Know-all.

smarty-boots *or* **-pants** Know-all.

smash
1. [adj.] Considerable. Usu. **smash hit** Great success.
2. [n.] Notably successful thing.

237

smashed
1. Strongly under the influence of drugs.
2. Drunk. Also **smashed out of one's mind** *or* **brains**.

smasher Extremely pleasing person or thing.

smashing Exceptionally pleasing.

smell [v.]
1. **get a smell at** Approach. Get close to.
2. Appear to be deserving of suspicion.

smeller Nose.

smog Mixture of fog and smoke in cities.

smoke Cigarette.

smoke, the London. Any big city.

smooch [v.] Embrace or caress amorously and lengthily.

smoothie Man with ostentatiously (perhaps insincerely) polite manners, behaviour and speech.

snaffle Steal. Appropriate. Annex without permission.

snap Packed meal (usu. for workman).

snap out of it Get rid of a mood, habit, etc.

snappy, make it Be quick about it.

snarl-up Entanglement (usu. traffic-jam). [Adj.] **snarled-up** Entangled. Broken down.

snatch [n.] Rapid robbery.

snazzy Smart. Fashionable.

sneak
1. [v.] Make off with. Steal.
2. [n.] Informer.
3. [v.] Inform against.

sneakers Shoes with soft, noiseless soles.

snide [adj.]
1. Indirectly offensive. Underhandedly unkind.
2. Counterfeit.
3. Contemptible. Mean.

sniffy Scornful. Contemptuous.

snifter Drink (usu. of spirits).

snip
1. Bargain.
2. Easy undertaking or success.

snitch
1. [n.] Nose.
2. [v.] Act as informer.
3. [v.] Steal.

snog [v.] & [n.] Embrace or caress amorously.

snook, cock a Show disrespect or contempt.

snooker [v.] Outwit. Place at disadvantage.

snoop Pry stealthily (esp. for breaches of law). Hence **snooper**.

snooty Haughty. Patronising.

snort [n.] Drink.

snorter
1. Anything of exceptional size, strength.
2. Very attractive person or thing.

snot* Nasal mucus.

snot-rag* Handkerchief.

snotty Huffy. Quick to take offence.

snotty-nosed Filthy.

snout
1. Tobacco. (Prison slang.)
2. Informer to police.

snow Cocaine. Thus **snow-bird** Cocaine addict.

snowball (or -flake) in hell, no more chance than a No chance at all. Also **not a snowball (or -flake) in hell's chance.**

snozzle Nose.

snuff it (or out) Die.

snuff, up to Experienced. Knowing.

snug Bar-parlour in public house.

snug as a bug in a rug Very comfortable.

snurdge Disagreeable person.

so-and-so
1. Expression used in place of a person's name when it cannot be remembered.
2. Disagreeable person. Polite evasion of such terms of abuse as **bugger, bastard**, etc.

so long Good-bye.

so what? What does it matter?

soak Charge or tax extortionately.

soap
1. Flattery. Usu. **soft soap**.
2. [v.] Flatter. Ingratiate.

soap opera Radio or television serial, often of trivial or sentimental nature. Also **soap**.

sob sister Woman journalist responsible for articles dealing with women's problems (usu. through correspondence columns in newspaper or magazine).

sob story Story intended to engage hearer's pity (e.g. for teller's bad luck) or emotions.

sob stuff Over-sentimentalised story, film, etc.

sock
1. [n.] Blow.
2. [v.] Strike. Deliver a blow at. Overwhelm.
3. **sock it to them** Liven them up.
4. **sock it to me, baby** Let us liven things up.

sock in it, put a Stop talking.

socko Outstanding success.

socks up, pull one's Be more efficient. Work harder.

sod*
1. Sodomite. [Abbr.]
2. Term of abuse for person or thing. (As with similar terms, e.g. **bastard, bugger**, can be amiable in some contexts, e.g.
   • *lucky sod*.)
3. **sod all** Nothing whatsoever.
4. **sod it!** Excl. of annoyance.
5. **sod off** Depart.

sodding* Adj. or adv. of vulgar emphasis. (E.g.
- *Not sodding likely.* No.)

soft
1. Foolish. Also **soft in the head**.
2. Easy. Also **soft option** Easy job.
3. **soft on** Affectionately disposed towards (a person). In love with.
4. **soft ha'porth** Person easily put on.
5. **soft number** Easy job.

soft sawder
1. [n.] Flattery.
2. [v.] Flatter.

soft sell Persuasive, discreet, almost diffident method of salesmanship.

soft soap
1. Flattery.
2. [v.] Flatter.

soft spot for, have a Be kindly disposed towards.

soft touch Person easily persuaded.

softy Weak-minded person.

soixante-neuf Sexual act involving simultaneous fellatio and cunnilingus.

sold down the river Tricked.

soldier
1. See **old soldier**.
2. **soldier on** Persevere in spite of difficulties.

solid Entire.
- *Twenty solid minutes.*

solitary Solitary confinement.

some
1. [adj.] Very praiseworthy.
   - *He's certainly some cricketer.*
2. Not much. **some hope!** You haven't much chance!
3. Adv. of emphasis. **going some** Going very quickly.
4. **and then some** And more in addition.

some mothers have em! Excl. of despair at folly of another.

something Emph. addition to an adj. or adv.
- *She suffers something awful from migraine.*

something about one, to have To have mildly attractive or fascinating qualities.

something good An enjoyable prospect.

something the cat's brought in, like Bedraggled.

son of a bitch Unpleasant fellow.

son of a gun Fellow.

song and dance
1. Fuss. Commotion.
2. **nothing to make a song (and dance) about** Trivial.

sonny
1. Affectionate or informal term of address to boy.
2. Offensive term of address to man.

soonish Quite soon. As soon as possible.

soppy Foolish. Foolishly sentimental.

sort Fellow. Usu. **a good sort** An obliging person.

sort of In a way. Somehow.

sort out [v.] Fight with. Pick quarrel with. Overwhelm. Bring order to. Punish. Deal with.

sort-out [n.] Process of tidying-up.

sorts, of Not quite deserving the name.

sou, not have a Be penniless.

sound off Lose one's temper. Express one's opinion forcibly.

soup and fish Evening dress.

soup, in the In difficulty.

souped-up (Of car) Made more powerful by adjustments or additions to engine.

sour-puss Glum person.

soused Drunk.

south-paw Left-handed boxer.

sozzled Drunk.

spaced-out Not in touch with reality.

spade Negro. [Derog.]

spank along Move briskly and smartly.

spanker Excellent person or thing.

spanking
1. [adj.] Brisk
   - *(A spanking breeze.)* Smartly attractive
   - *(A spanking woman.)* Rapid
   - *(A spanking pace.)* Large. Showy. Extremely pleasing.
2. [adv.] Very.

spare
1. Very angry. Usu. **go spare** Become very angry.
2. Idle. not wanted.
3. **spare prick*** Incompetent person.
4. **standing about like a spare prick*** Standing idle. (Of people.)
5. **spare tyre** Fatness round person above waist.

spark See **bright spark**.

sparklers Diamonds.

sparks Radio operator.

sparrer Sparrow.

spat [n.] Quarrel, usu. trivial.

speak-easy Place where drink is illegally sold.

spec, on Without making advance arrangements. Hoping for chance success.

specimen Fellow (usu. derog.).

speck Place from which one is a spectator (at football match, etc.) e.g. **a good speck** A good position from which to view.

specs Spectacles.

speed Amphetamine drug.

speed-cop Policeman checking motorists' speed.

speed-merchant
1. Person who drives at high speed.
2. Person who acts or moves quickly.

spend a penny Go to the lavatory.

spew (up) one's guts *or* **ring** Vomit violently.

spice Lubricious content in film, play, magazine, etc.

spiel Speech. Story. Patter. (Often glib and rehearsed, as of salesmen, tramps, etc.) [v.] Speak thus. [n.] **spieler** One who speaks thus. Also professional swindler.

spiffing Very good.

spiflicate Treat (person) roughly (usu. in vague threat).

spike
1. [v.] Reject an unwanted contribution (journalistic).
2. [n.] Hypodermic needle.
3. **spike one's drink** Add extra alcohol to one's drink.

spiky Having rigorous and uncompromising attitude (usu. High Church).

spill
1. Confess.
2. **spill a bibful** Blab.

spill the beans *or* **works** Give information (usu. unintentionally or unwillingly).

spin See **flat spin**.

spin-off [n.] By-product (usu. of commercially successful entertainments; e.g. full-length feature film based on characters in popular television series; toys, etc. based on popular TV programmes).

spit and a drag *or* **draw** Smoke (usu. furtive because unauthorised).

spit and sawdust [Lit.] Public-house bar with sawdust on floor and customers prone to spitting. [Met.] Any unpretentious place of entertainment, restaurant, etc. Usu. adj.
● *It's a bit spit and sawdust.* It's a place in simple taste.

spit it out Say what you have to say.

spitting feathers Having a dry throat. Thirsty.

spitting image Exact likeness. (Incorrect for 'Spit and image'.)

spiv Person, often flashily dressed, who makes a living by exercise of wits rather than working (usu. by selling goods illegally or semi-legally acquired, by touting, or on fringe of shady activities, often in racing circles).

splash
1. **have a splash** *or* **splash one's boots** Urinate. (Men only.)
2. Ostentation. Display. Excitement. Sensation.
3. Small quantity of water etc. added to spirits.
4. [v.] Spend money extravagantly. Usu. **splash out**. [n.] Extravagant expenditure.

splattered, get Be heavily defeated.

splendiferous Splendid [emph.].

splice Join in marriage.

split Leave. Depart.

split (on) Betray secrets (of), e.g. to police.

split (with) Quarrel with and part permanently (from).

splodgy Blotchy. Discoloured. Of mixed colour.

splosh, go Fall noisily into water.

splurge [n.] Prominent display. Lavish expenditure. Also [v.].

spoil the ship for a ha'porth of tar Ruin an entire enterprise, or fail to complete a task properly, because of minor parsimony.

spondulicks Money. (Various spellings.)

spoof
1. [n.] & [v.] Hoax. Trick. Cheat.
2. [adj.] Bogus.

spoon [v.] Flirt (usu. in over-sentimental way).

sport
1. [n.] Good fellow, willing to enter into the spirit of a game, contest, activity, etc. without concern for dignity, defeat, etc.
2. Term of address. [Facet.] Also **old sport**.

spot
1. Small amount.
2. Difficulty. Usu. **in a (tight) spot** In trouble.

    3. [v.] Forecast. Catch sight of.
    4. **on the spot** Alert.

spot of, a A little.

spot on Very accurate. Exact(ly).

spotted dick *or* **dog** Plum-duff.

spout, up the In pawn. Ruined (of plans, etc.).

spread
    1. [n.] Feast.
    2. [v.] Spread oneself. Spare no expense or effort.

spring Arrange escape usu. of person from prison.

sprog Recruit. Hence, new boy at school.

spud
    1. Potato.
    2. **spud-bashing** Potato-peeling.
    3, **spud-basher** Potato-peeler.

spunk
    1. Courage.
    2. Semen.

spunky Spirited.

squaddy Soldier.

square
    1. [adj.] Conventional, traditional, staid, honest, decent. Old-fashioned, reactionary.
    2. [n.] Person having these qualities.
    3. **on the square** Honest. Honestly.
    4. [v.] Bribe. Pay.

square-bashing Military drill or training.

square-eyes Avid watcher of TV.

square-head German.

square one, back to Back to the beginning. Back to where we were some time ago.

square peg Misfit.

squat
1. Move into a deserted house and live there illegally.
2. **squatter** One who does this.
3. [n.] Place where squatters live.

squeak Inform to authorities.

squeal
1. Inform to authorities, esp. police.
2. [n.] **squeal(er)** One who does this.
3. Protest excitedly.

squeeze-box Concertina; piano-accordion.

squiffy Drunk.

squint Glance.

squirt Disagreeable person (usu. both self-assertive and insignificant).

squit Same as **squirt**.

squitters Diarrhoea. Also **squits**.

stab [n.] Attempt. Usu. **have a stab at**.

stack, blow one's Become very angry.

stack cards Shuffle pack of cards dishonestly. Hence, take an unfair advantage.
* *The cards are stacked against him.* The odds are against his success.

stacks Large quantities.

staggers, the Inability to walk normally (usu. because of intoxication).

stake out Place under surveillance.

stamping-ground District frequented (or formerly frequented) by one. Place well known to one because of social connexions. Area where one lives, works or is well known socially, etc.

stand
1. [n.] Erection of penis.
2. Tolerate.
3. See **racket**.

stand-by Not reserved in advance.

stand one's hand Pay whole (or one's personal share) of bill.

stand up Keep waiting. Fail to meet as arranged.

standing on one's head See **head, do something . . .**

stark-bollock naked* Naked.

stark raving mad Very angry or crazy. See also **bonkers**.

starkers Stark naked.

starry-eyed Over-idealistic. Unpractical. Infatuatedly in love.

start a hare Begin a fresh and usu. irrelevant line of enquiry or discussion.

starters, for To begin with.

start on Bully. Upbraid.

start something Set in train something likely to have significant or surprising results.

starve Feel hungry.

stash
1. Put away.
2. **stashed away** Hidden away; (of money) in a bank account.

state Condition of untidiness, anxiety, excitement, etc. Usu. **in a state**.

stay, has come to Must be regarded as permanent. Also **is here to stay**.

stay put Remain in position.

stayer One who persists in an undertaking.

steady See **go steady**.

steam along Make good progress.

steam radio Sound radio (as opposed to TV).

steamed up Indignant.

steaming Indignant.

steep
1. Extremely high (of prices, etc.).
2. Difficult to believe (of stories, etc.).

step on it *or* **the gas** Go more quickly.

stew Disagreeable position (usu. of perplexity).

stick
1. [n.] Dull or awkward person. Usu. **old stick** *or* **dry old stick**.
2. **the stick** Beating with a stick.
3. [v.] Endure. Tolerate. Also **stick it (out), stick at it** Persist.
4. See **stuck**.
5. [Abbr.] **stick of furniture** Piece of furniture.
6. **get some stick** Receive harsh criticism, scolding, vigorous encouragement.
7. See **wrong end of the stick**.
8. **give some stick** Provide impetus, force, drive, power. Encourage. Scold.
9. [v.] Put in position. Remain in place
   • (*I'll stick where I am*).

stick it (up his jumper, etc.**), he can** I don't care what he (etc.) does with it (whatever is being referred to) because I have no further interest in the matter.

stick to Remain faithful to. Retain.

stick out
1. Be prominent. Often **stick out a mile** *or* **like a sore thumb** Be very obvious.
2. **stick out for** Insist on.
3. **stick one's neck out** Take a risk. Invite criticism or trouble by being provocative, out-spoken, etc.

stick up [v.] Rob by threatening with violence.

stick-up [n.] Robbery by threat of violence, usu. at gunpoint (the victim being required to 'stick up' his hands (*stick 'em up*) in the air).

stick up for Defend. Support.

stick up to Oppose.

stickability Persistence. Endurance.

sticker Same as **stayer**.

sticks Cricket stumps. Hurdles (in racing). Goal posts. Rural areas.

sticky

    1. Unpleasant. Also **a sticky end**. A disagreeable form of death or ruin.

    2. See **wet and sticky**.

    3. **bat on a sticky wicket** Function in difficult circumstances.

stiff

    1. [n.] Corpse.

    2. [n.] Term of mild abuse, but very often facet. Often **big stiff**.

    3. **stiff with** Crowded with. Well provided with.

    4. [adv.] Considerably.

       • *Bored stiff; scared stiff.*

sting

    1. [v.] Swindle. Usu. **stung** Swindled.

    2. Charge.

stink

    1. [n.] Unpleasant or scandalous revelation. Complaint. Fuss.

    2. **kick up a stink** Make a great fuss. Also **raise a stink**.

    3. [v.] Be obnoxious, unacceptable.

    4. **like stink** Very fast, energetically. Intensely.

    5. **stink of money** Be very rich.

stinker

    1. Unpleasant person.

    2. Difficult problem, undertaking, etc.

    3. Strongly worded document (complaint, letter, criticism, etc.).

stinking

    1. Considerably and obnoxiously.

       • *Stinking rich, drunk,* etc.

    2. Obnoxious. Very disagreeable.

       • *A stinking cold.*

    3. Strongly worded (complaint, letter, criticism, etc.).

    4. **stinking with** Having much (usu. money).

stir [n.] Prison.

stir it (up) Make trouble or fuss.

stir one's stumps Hurry.

stirrer Trouble-maker.

stitch someone up Arrange matter or affairs so as to defeat someone.

stitches, in Laughing uncontrollably.

stockbroker belt District inhabited by wealthy people in large houses (usu. in countryside near city).

stodge Heavy or fattening food, such as suet-pudding.

stoke up Eat.

stone cold sober Very sober.

stone me! *or* **the crows!** Excl. of surprise, disgust, etc.

stoned
   1. Very drunk.
   2. Under the influence of drugs.
   3. **stoned out of one's mind** Very much under the influence of intoxicants.

ston(e)y(-broke) Penniless.

stooge
   1. [n.] Butt for comedian, i.e. one who asks questions which comedian answers, etc.
   2. Person easily imposed on. Subordinate carrying out simple work.
   3. [v.] **stooge around** Wander aimlessly about. Wait.

stook, in Short of money. In difficulty.

stool pigeon Informer to police.

stop Receive (blow etc.).

stop a clock, enough to Ugly.

stop-go [adj.] Of intermittent progress, development, activity, improvement, etc.
   ● *Stop-go policy in economic expansion.*

stop off at Call in on (person) or at (place).

stop over
   1. [v.] Visit briefly (usu. for a night).
   2. [n.] **stop-over** Brief visit. Temporary halt during journey.

stop the show Be a great success (usu. of person attracting so much applause as to hold up a performance temporarily).

stork Traditional bringer of new babies.

story Lie.

stout fellow Worthy fellow.

stow it Stop it. Be quiet.

strafe [n.] & [v.] Attack. (Military.)

straight
1. **go straight** Behave honestly (following period of crime or in prison, etc.).
2. [Excl.] Honestly!
3. **on the straight** Behaving honestly.
4. **straight as a dog's hind (or back) leg** Crooked.
5. (Of spirits) Undiluted.
6. [adj.] Not homosexual.

straight as they make them Very honest.

straight from the horse's mouth Authoritative. Authentic (of information).

straight-up
1. Correct.
2. [Excl.] Honestly!

straight up and down
1. Honest.
2. Easy.

straighten out Correct. Punish. Reprimand severely. Put right.

strap, on (the) On credit.

strapped Short of money.

streak
1. [n.] Thin person. **(long) streak of misery** Thin, morose person.
2. [v.] Run in public place while indecently unclothed. Hence **streaker**.
3. **like a streak** Very quickly.

street See **Queer Street**.

street (as), not in the same Inferior (to).

street, up one's One's concern, speciality or taste. Also **right (or bang) up one's street** Very much to one's taste, liking; very much the thing one is good at.

streets ahead (of) Far superior (to).

stretch Period of imprisonment.

strewth! Excl. of disgust or annoyance.

strike a light! Excl. of surprise or annoyance.

strike all of a heap Astound.

strike lucky Enjoy a piece of luck.

strike me pink! Excl. of surprise.

string along
1. Cooperate. Usu. **string along with**.
2. Inveigle. Hoax. Deceive.

string, on a In suspense.

string up Kill by hanging.

stringer Newspaper reporter paid only for those contributions which are published, e.g. provincial full-time journalist receiving extra payments for occasional contributions to national press.

strings attached Disadvantages. Restrictions. Modifications. Qualifications.

strings, pull Exert personal influence.

strip off See **tear a strip off**.

stroll on! Mild excl. of despair.

strong
1. **going strong** Continuing vigorously.
2. **come it strong** Speak strongly. Exaggerate.

strong on
1. Good at.
2. Setting great store by.

stroppy Obstreperous.

struck all of a heap Rendered speechless, nonplussed, astonished.

struck on Attracted by.

stuck At a halt (usu. because puzzled).

stuck for Lacking.

stuck in (*or* into it), get Work hard. Make serious start on something. Also invitation to eat or drink.

stuck on Captivated by.

stuck with Left (reluctantly) in possession of.

stud Promiscuous man. Male prostitute.

stuff
1. Word used widely in place of many nouns which the speaker cannot remember or identify.
2. **bit of stuff** Sexually attractive woman.
3. **the hard stuff** Spirits (usu. whisky). Money.
4. See **hot stuff, rough stuff**.
5. [v.] Copulate with.*
6. Hashish. Heroin.
7. Defeat.
8. Keep.
   • *I don't want his apologies: he can stuff them.*

stuff, do one's Do that which one is good at or has to do.

stuff, know one's Be good at one's trade, etc.

stuff to give the troops, the Exactly what is required. Also **that's the stuff to give 'em**.

stuffed, get Dismissive expression of no precise meaning but with contemptuous implications.
• *He can go and get stuffed.* I wish to have nothing to do with him.

stuffed shirt Conceited idiot.

stuffing out of, knock the
1. Beat severely. Defeat. Weaken.
2. Sadden considerably.
   • *His death knocked the stuffing out of her.*

stumblebum Foolish person, esp. one prone to blunder.

stumer
1. Fool.
2. **come a stumer** Fall heavily [lit.] & [met.].
3. Anything worthless.

stump See **stir one's stumps**.

stump, on the Making political speech, esp. during tour.

stump up Pay.

stumped At a loss. Nonplussed.

stung Swindled. Charged extortionately.

stunner Very attractive, delightful person or thing.

stunning Splendid. Superlatively good.

stunt
1. Showy or sensational feat, trick, device, dodge, novel idea or similar undertaking (usu. to attract publicity).
2. **stunt-man** Person employed to replace actors in filming of dangerous scenes involving e.g. falls, crashes, etc.

sub
1. Abbr. of subscription, substitute, subaltern, submarine, sub-edit.
2. [n.] & [v.] Loan (money).

suck-hole [n.] & [v.] Toady.

suck up to Fawn servilely on.

sucker Gullible person.

sucks (boo) to you Excl. of derisive triumph. [Juv.]

sudden death [n.] & [adj.] Appl. to sporting fixtures where the first score wins (e.g. in golf, when extra play is necessary following a drawn game).

suffering cats! Mild excl. of annoyance or surprise.

sugar Familiar term of address to woman.

sugar daddy Middle-aged or elderly man acting as protector, source of revenue or of generous gifts, for younger woman.

summat Something.

sundowner Early evening drink.

sunshine Familiar term of address.

sun shines out of one's backside *or* **arsehole,* think the** Be very devoted to one (or oneself).

sunk Defeated. Ruined. Finished.

255

super
1. Superintendent. [Abbr.]
2. [n.] Extra (i.e. person with small part or in crowd in film or play). Supernumerary. [Abbr.]
3. [adj.] Excellent. Also **super-duper**.

superstar Specially well-known entertainer.

sure!
1. [Excl.] Certainly! With pleasure! Also **sure thing**!
2. **for sure** Indubitably.
3. Undoubtedly.

sure as eggs is eggs, as Without any doubt. Also **as sure as God made little apples**.

sure-fire Certain.

sure, that's for That is certain.

surface [v.] Wake up.

sus, suss
1. Suspicion. Suspect. [Abbr. Police and criminal only.] Hence **on sus** On suspicion.
2. **to be sussed** To be held for questioning on suspicion. To be found out.
3. [v.] Discover. Usu. **sus out** Find out (for oneself).

swad(dy) Soldier.

swag Booty.

swagger [adj.] Smart. Fashionable. Showy.

swan [v.] Move aimlessly. Also **swan about** *or* **around**.

swank
1. [n.] Showing off. Conceited behaviour. Swagger.
2. [v.] Behave in this way.
3. **swank(y)** [adj.] Showy.
4. **swank(-pot)** One who behaves in this way. Also **swanker**.

swap [n.] & [v.] Exchange.

swear by Have belief in.

sweat
1. [n.] Hard work. State of anxiety.
2. **old sweat** Experienced person, often old soldier.
3. **sweat it out** Persevere despite difficulty, pressure, etc.

sweat on Expect anxiously. Anticipate eagerly. Esp. **sweating on** In state of (nervous) hope.

sweat one's guts out Work very hard.

sweeny, the (Of police) The Flying Squad.

sweet fanny adams *or* **FA** See **FA**.

sweet on, be Be fond of.

sweeten Bribe. Also [n.] **sweetener**.

sweetie
1. Sweetmeat. [Juv.]
2. Term of familiar address to woman. [Abbr.] Sweetheart.
3. Kind, considerate, attractive person (usu. young woman).

swell
1. [n.] Person of distinction or fashionable appearance. Also [adj.] Having such qualities.
2. [adj.] Excellent.

swell-head Conceited person. [adj.] **swell-headed**.

swelled head, have a Be conceited. [adj.] **swelled-headed**. Also **swollen head**.

s'welp me (god)! Excl. of surprise or asseveration.

swig [n.] & [v.] Drink.

swill [n.] & [v.] Wash.

swim like a brick Swim badly. Sink.

swing
1. Be hanged.
2. **swing it** Arrange it by exerting influence.
3. **take a swing at** Aim a blow at. Punch.
4. Play jazz music well.
5. Behave in a **swinging** fashion.

swing the lead
1. Avoid work.
2. Boast.

swinger Fashionable person. [Pop.]

swinging Lively, fashionable, progressive. [Pop.]

swipe [v.] Steal.

swish Luxurious. Smart. Fashionable.

switched on
1. Alert. Up to date.
2. Under the influence of drugs.

swivel-eyed git Term of abuse.

swiz(zle) [n.] Swindle. Hoax.

swop Same as **swap**.

swot
1. [n.] Person who studies (unpopularly) hard.
2. [v.] Study (usu. in preparation for exam). Also **swot up**.

sync [Abbr.] Synchronisation. Synchronise.

T

TB Tuberculosis.

TGIF Thank God it's Friday.

ta! Thanks!

ta-ra *or* **-ta** Good-bye.

tabs on, keep Maintain a check on.

tackle
1. [n.] Equipment. Clothes. Belongings.
2. [v.] Attempt. Grapple with. Attack. Speak to (a person about something).

Taff(y) Welshman.

tag along Go or accompany (usu. in subordinate capacity).

tail
1. [n.] Sexual enjoyment. Sexually attractive woman.
2. [v.] Follow closely; shadow.

tail, be (*or* get) on one's Be in search of one in order to scold or recriminate.

tail-back Long queue of traffic.

tail-end Charlie Last person in a succession.

tail-gate [v.] Drive (dangerously) close to vehicle in front.

tails Tail coat and full evening dress.

take Overtake.

take a dim view (of) Disapprove (of).

take a knock Suffer a loss (usu. financial).

take all one's time Tax all one's powers.

take a running jump (at oneself), (go and) Go to hell.

take-away
1. Shop or restaurant selling ready-cooked food for customers to eat off premises.
2. Meal thus prepared and sold.

take for a ride Mislead. Cause (a person) protracted and deliberate trouble.

take in Visit.

take it Endure bravely and without complaint.

take it on the chin Accept without evasion.

take it with you, you can't You may as well enjoy your personal possessions, since they are of no use after your death.

take on Grieve.

take one's hooks Depart.

take the biscuit *or* **cake** Surpass everything (usu. in effrontery, unpleasantness, etc.).

take the can back Same as **carry the can**.

take the piss (out of)* Make fun (of), objectionably.

take the weight off one's feet Sit down.

taken short In urgent need of the lavatory.

talent Attractive men or girls.

talk down to Talk in a manner appropriate for audience of simpler understanding.

talking, now you're That is closer to the point.

talk the hind (*or* back) leg(s) off a donkey Talk excessively or very fluently.

talk through one's hat Boast, bluff, exaggerate, talk nonsense.

talk through the back of one's neck Talk nonsense.

talk to Rebuke. Same as **give one a talking to**.

talk turkey Tell the plain truth. Talk sense.

talk wet See **wet**.

talk, you can You are no better yourself.

tall order Excessive or demanding undertaking or request.

tall story Exaggerated or incredible tale.

tan (one's hide) Thrash (one severely).

tank along Go fast. (Of car.)

tanked (up) Full of intoxicating drink.

tap [v.] Same as **bug (2)**.

tap (person) for Apply to (person) for (money).

tap, on Readily available at any time.

taped
1. Understand. (Of person) Estimated and judged.
2. Arranged. Settled.

tapper One who fits secret listening device in telephone, room, etc. in order to overhear private conversation.

tar Sailor.

tar-brush, have a touch (*or* lick) of the* Be of African or Asian descent.

tar(r)adiddle Petty lie.

tart Young woman of loose or apparently loose morals. See **tart up**.

tart up
1. Brighten up, decorate (usu. cheaply, flashily or super-ficially).
2. Dress (oneself) like a **tart** (often facet.). Smarten up.

tarty Vulgarly decorated. Behaving or looking like a **tart**.

tash Moustache.

tasty Sexually attractive.

tat [n.] [Lit.] Rags. [Met.] Something messy, untidy, disorgan-ised. See **tatty**.

tater Potato.

tatty Messy, inferior, cheap, in poor taste, of poor standard.

tear a strip off Reprimand.

tear-jerker Film, play, etc., of sentimental nature.

tease [n.] Person fond of teasing.

teaser Problem.

Tech College of Technology.

ted Young ruffian. See **teddy boy**.

teddy boy Youth affecting clothing reminiscent of Edwardian period. [Old f.] Gen., a young ruffian or **spiv**. [Abbr.] **ted.**

tee up Arrange, plan, prepare. **teed up** Ready.

teeny-bopper Young (i.e. aged about 11–14) devotee of popular music, fashion, etc.

teeny(-weeny) Tiny. Also **teensy-weensy**.

teeth, kick in the Treat (person) with contempt.

tell on Reveal facts about.

tell one where one gets off Scold one.

tell that to the marines! Do you expect me to believe that!

tell t'other from which Distinguish between two things or persons.

tell you what, (I) (I'll) I'll tell you something.

telling me, you're I know that already.

telly Television.

temp Temporary secretary, typist, office-assistant, etc.

temperament, throw a Have an angry outburst.

tenner, a £10 (note).

terms (with), (get) on (Improve one's performance so that one is) at a standard appropriate (to) (one's competitors, e.g. in a game).

terrible Considerable.
  • *A terrible nuisance, etc.* Incompetent.

terribly Very greatly.
  • *Terribly worried*, etc.

terrific Excessive. Very considerable.
* *A terrific fuss.* [Adv.] **terrifically.**

terror, holy Considerable nuisance. (Of person only.)

that'll be the day! That will never happen!

that there That.

thick
1. Friendly. **thick as thieves** Very friendly to one another.
2. Unfair. Unpleasant.
3. **a thick ear** [Lit.] A blow on the ear (usu. in threat) e.g.
   * *You'll get a thick ear).* [Met.] Rebuff (usu. facet.).
4. **lay it on thick** Exaggerate. Flatter.
5. **a bit thick** Unreasonable.
6. Stupid. **thick as two short planks** Very stupid.

thin
1. Disappointing. Usu. **have a thin time** Be unsuccessful, or in a disappointing period.
2. **thin on the ground** Sparse.

thing
1. The fashion.
2. The socially acceptable custom.
3. **a thing about** An antipathy to. A fad or obsession about.
4. **do one's own thing** Do what one enjoys doing.

thingummy(bob) *or* **(jig)** Thing or person one cannot remember the name of.

thingy Thing.

think, have a Spend time in thinking.

think, I don't Phrase added to ironical statement.

think-tank Group of persons brought together to think, plan, etc.

think up Devise by thinking.

thinking-cap, put on one's Reflect.

this here This. [Emph.]

this is where we came in This is where we started. (Said when argument returns to starting-point, etc.)

thou Thousand.

thrash Party. Bout of heavy drinking.

three sheets in the wind Drunk. Also **three parts cut**.

through, be
1. Be finished.
2. **be through with** Refuse to have anything more to do with.

throw [v.] Disconcert.

throw, a Each.
- *The tickets were £1 a throw.*

throw a fit Become very angry.

throw a party Give a party.

throw one's weight about Behave overbearingly. Use one's authority.

throw the book at Reprimand severely.

throw up Vomit.

thumbs up Indication of victory, success or cheerfulness. Hence **get (give) the thumbs up** Receive (give) approval, esp. to begin something. Opp. **thumbs down**.

thump [v.] Defeat.

thump, is it It is not. [Emph.]

thumping (great) Very large or heavy.

thunder, what in *or* **the** *or* **in the name of** What. [Emph.]

thundering Immense. Very great. Remarkable.

tich Small person. Also **tichy** Very small.

tick
1. Disagreeable person.
2. **on tick** On credit.
3. Moment.
   - *Half a tick. Please wait two ticks.*
4. [v.] Function.
   - *I don't know what makes him tick.* I do not understand how his mind, personality (etc.) works.

tick off Reprimand.

ticker [n.]
1. Watch.
2. Heart.

ticket, the The right thing (to do). That which is needed.
- *That's just the ticket.*

tickety-boo Satisfactory.

tickled pink *or* **to death** Delighted. Amused.

tiddler
1. Stickleback.
2. Small person or thing.

tiddling Very small.

tiddly
1. (Slightly) drunk.
2. Very small.

tide-mark Line between washed and unwashed parts of person's face, neck or body.

tidy Considerable.

tied up
1. (Of person.) Occupied. Busy.
2. (Of arrangements, plans, etc.) Satisfactorily prepared.

tight
1. Mean. Also **tight-arsed.***
2. Difficult. Hence **tight spot**. Difficult personal situation.
3. **tightwad** Mean person.
4. Drunk. Also **tight as a drum** *or* **newt** *or* **tick** Very drunk.
5. **sit tight** Remain where one is. Wait.

tike Contemptible person.

tile Hat.

tile loose, have a Be slightly crazy.

tiles, on the On a spree (usu. of drinking).

till the cows come home For a very long time. Indefinitely.

time, do Serve a prison-sentence.

time, in (less than) no Very quickly.

timer, old Experienced person in job, profession, etc.

tin hat Soldier's steel helmet.

tin lid on it, that's put the That is a serious set-back, which may have put an end to everything.

tin Lizzie Cheap motor-car.

Tin Pan Alley Area off Charing Cross Road frequented by writers, performers and publishers of popular music.

tin-pot Unimportant. Inferior. Cheap.

tinies Small children.

tinkle Urinate. Urination.

tinkle, give a Telephone.

tip off [v.] Give information to (usu. privately).

tip-off [n.] Hint.

tip (one) the wink Warn (one), often surreptitiously.

tipple
1. [v.] Fall heavily. (Of rain.)
2. [n.] Drink (usu. alcoholic).

tiswas See **all of a tiswas**.

tit*
1. Mammary nipple. Breast.
2. Button which has to be pressed to operate machines, etc.
3. **get on one's tit(s)** Annoy, irritate one.
4. **look an absolute** *or* **right tit** Appear foolish.
5. **tit show** Entertainment with display of partially-clothed ladies.
6. Ineffectual or foolish person.

titch See **tich**.

titfer Hat.

tittie See **titty**.

titty Breast.

tizz(y) State of confusion or excitement. Also **tizwas**.

toast, on Readily available. At one's mercy.

tod, on one's Alone.

toddle Depart.

toe-rag Beggar.

toes, tread on one's Annoy one (usu. by indiscreet action infringing one's prerogatives).

toes, turn up one's Die.

toff Same as **swell (1)**.

toffed up Smartly dressed.

toffee, for At all.
- *I can't sing for toffee.* I cannot sing at all.

toffee-nosed Haughty.

togged up Dressed smartly.

togs Clothes.

toing and froing Moving about.

tommy British Army private.

tommy rot Nonsense.

tomorrow, like there's With no regard for what the consequences might be.

ton, the One hundred (e.g. miles per hour).

ton-up boy Member of young gang of motor-cyclists.

ton of bricks See **like a ton**.

tongue, give someone (*or* feel) the rough edge of one's Administer (or receive) reprimand.

tonk [v.] Hit.

tons (of) Plenty (of).

too big for one's boots Boastful. Conceited.

too (bloody, etc.) true Emph. expression of agreement.

too funny for words Extremely amusing.

too much of a good thing Unacceptably excessive.

toodle-oo Good-bye.

tool
1. [n.] Penis.*
2. [v.] Move aimlessly. **tool along, about, around, etc.** Move (walk, drive) without purpose. Be unoccupied.

tootle off Depart.

tootsies Toes.

top
1. See **over the top**.
2. [v.] Hang.
3. **from the top** From the beginning.

top brass Officers. Senior officials in any organisation.

top dog Victor. Master.

top drawer, (out of the) Upper class.

top hat on it, that's put the Same as **tin lid**.

top-hole First class. (Old f., therefore facet.)

top-notch Very good.

topper
1. Top hat.
2. Excellent person.

topping Excellent.

tops, the The best.

torn it, that's That is a serious set-back.

tosh
1. Nonsense.
2. Familiar term of address.

toss, not give a (monkey's*) Not care in the slightest.

toss off* Masturbate. [n.] **toss-off.**

toss-pot Term of abuse applied to person.

tot Small amount of drink (usu. spirits).

tote Totalisator (official machine for recording and paying out bets on racecourse).

totter [n.] Rag-and-bone man.

tottie
1. Same as **crumpet**.
2. Pretty girl.

totting Collecting valuable items from refuse.

touch
1. [v.] Cadge from.
   - *He touched me for £1*. He obtained £1 from me.
2. [n.] Person from whom one can readily cadge or obtain something.
   - *A soft touch*. Too generous a person.

touch lucky Have a stroke of luck.

touch of the tar-brush, have a* Be of African or Asian origin.

touch up Caress sexually.

tough
1. [n.] Violent criminal. Ruffian.
2. [adj.] Severe. Hard.
   - *Tough luck*.
   - *It's rather tough on him*. It's rather unpleasant for him.
3. **get tough with** Act sternly towards.

tracks
1. See **make tracks**.
2. **in one's tracks** Where one stands. There and then.
   - *The discovery stopped them in their tracks*.

trad Traditional.

trainers Running shoes.

traipse Go (usu. aimlessly, wearily).

tram-stopper Very thick sandwich.

tranklements Belongings.

tranny Transistor radio.

transmogrify Transform.

trap [n.] Mouth.

trapes See **traipse**.

travel Move quickly.

treat, a (fair) [adv.] Very well indeed. Esp. **go down a treat** Succeed splendidly.

trendy Fashionable (usu. in intellectual, sociological or artistic matters). Also [n.] One who is thus fashionable, often with implication of superficiality.

trick cyclist Psychiatrist.

trick, do the Accomplish one's purpose.

tricks, how's How are things?

trigger off Cause. Set in motion a succession of events. Release pent-up feelings.

trip
1. [n.] Experience of drug-taking.
2. [v.] Take drugs.
3. [n.] **tripper** Drug-taker.

tripe Rubbish (spoken, written, etc.).

tripe-hound Disagreeable person.

trog Dull, conventionally-minded person.

troll Go.

trollybobs Trousers.

trot
1. Go.
2. **on the trot** In succession.

Trot Trotskyist. Person of strong left-wing views.

trotters Feet.

trouble, ask for Behave rashly.

trouble, get into (Cause to) become pregnant while unmarried.

trouble-shooter Person appointed to mediate or negotiate in industrial disputes as public relations expert.

trousers down, (catch) with one's (Catch) unawares.

trout, old Disagreeable (old) woman.

trowel, with a Excessively. Usu. **lay it on with a trowel** Flatter grossly.

trumps, turn up Do exactly what is required. Enjoy good fortune.

trust him (etc.) **as far as I could throw him** *or* **spit, I wouldn't** I do not trust him at all.

try it (*or* **something**) **on (with)** Attempt to deceive or impose on (person).

try-on [n.] Attempt to deceive or impose.

tub Fat person.

tub-thumper Ranting orator or preacher.

tuck
1. Food, esp. sweets and delicacies. (Usu. school slang.)
2. **tuck away** *or* **in** Eat heartily.

tum (-tum) Same as **tummy**.

tumble to Understand.

tummy Stomach.

tuppenny-ha'penny
1. Trivial. Inferior.
2. See **twopenny**.

turd* Contemptible person.

turf out Eject.

turn [n.] Nervous shock. Usu. **give one quite a turn** Administer slight shock to one.

turn in Go to bed.

turn it in *or* **up!**
1. Stop doing that!
2. Stop talking.

turn off Cause to lose interest.

turn on
1. Excite. Inspire. Interest.
2. Introduce to drugs. [adj.] **turned on**.
3. **turn it on** Provide an excellent display (e.g. of skill, by football team).

turn on the heat Exert pressure.

turn over Search.

turn up [v.] Cause to vomit.

turn-up [n.] Stroke of luck. Often **turn-up for the book** Lucky occurrence.

turned off Indifferent or hostile towards.

twaddle Nonsense.

twat*
1. Female private parts.
2. Fool.

twee Affectedly dainty.

twerp Fool.

twicer Cheat.

twig [v.] Understand.

twist
1. [n.] & [v.] Swindle.
2. **round the twist** Crazy.

twister
1. Swindler.
2. Puzzle.

twit Fool.

twitchy Nervous. Irritated. Suspicious.

twizzle [v.] Twirl.

two halfpennies to rub together, not have Be very poor.

two i/c [n.] Second-in-command.

twopenny damn, not care (*or*** give) a** Not care at all.

two-time Deceive.

tyke Yorkshireman. Also same as **tike**.

type Sort of person.

U

u/s Useless.

umpty Slightly unwell.

um(p)teen Large but undefined number. [adj.] **um(p)teenth.**

'un One.

unbeknownst to Without the knowledge of.

uncool Tense. Unpleasant.

under-dog
1. Person at a disadvantage. Often, person or team unlikely to win game, etc.
2. Person in subordinate position.

under the influence Drunk.

under the umbrella of Under the heading of. Under the protection or patronage of.

under the weather Unwell.

undies Underwear.

unearthly Preposterous.

unflappable Unperturbable.

ungodly Preposterous.

unholy Considerable.

unmentionables Trousers. Underwear.

unputdownable (of book) Engrossing. (Of person) Impossible to subdue.

unstuck, come Go wrong.

up
1. [v.] Begin abruptly to do or say something.
   - *He upped and went.*
   - Raise. *He upped with his fist.*
2. Ready.
   - *Tea up!*

Up against
1. Contending with.
2. **up against it** In serious difficulty.

up and coming Making one's reputation.

up and down, (straight) Straightforward.

up and downer Quarrel (usu. severe but verbal).

up and up, on the Improving.

up in Instructed or informed in.

up one's sleeve Ready for use.

up the pole
1. In difficulties. In a state of confusion.
2. Crazy.

up-tight Neurotically tense. Angry.

up to here, have it Be intensely irritated.

up to much, not Not very satisfactory.

up you(rs)!* Excl. of contemptuous rejoinder.

upper and a downer, an Same as **up and downer**.

upper crust [adj.] Of the higher levels of society. Also [n.].

uppers Amphetamine drug.

uppers, (down) on one's In destitute circumstances. Having bad fortune.

uppity Pert. Haughty. Cheeky.

ups Amphetamine drug.

ups-a-daisy! See **oops-a-daisy!**

27527575

upstairs See **kick upstairs**.

uptake, slow (etc.) **on the** Slow (etc.) to understand.

useful (Of person.) Capable.

usual, as per As usual.

V

VIP Very Important Person.

vac
1. Holiday.
2. Vacuum cleaner.

vamoose Depart. (Various spellings.)

vamp
1. [n.] Consciously seductive woman. Adventuress.
2. [v.] To behave as such.

varsity University.

veg Vegetables.

very devil, like the Very quickly or energetically.

vet
1. [n.] Veterinary surgeon.
2. [v.] Examine.

vetting Examination.

vibes Same as **vibrations**.

vibrations Atmosphere. Reactions to music, drugs, etc. [Pop.]

view See **dim view**.

villain Criminal.

-ville Added to various nouns and adjectives to signify atmosphere, event, situation, etc. having the quality of the noun or adjective. Hence, e.g., **swingsville** A **swinging** function [Pop.].

virgin bloody Mary Tomato juice.

vital statistics Measurements of woman's bust, waist and hips.

viva Oral examination.

W

WPB
1. Waste-paper basket.
2. [v.] Put in waste-paper basket.

wack(er) Term of address. (Liverpool only.)

wacky Unusual. Crazy.

wad
1. Roll of bank-notes.
2. Bun. Bread-roll sandwich.

wade into Attack vigorously.

wadge Mass. Bundle (of documents). Slice (of cake).

waffle
1. [n.] Verbiage. Nonsense.
2. [v.] Talk wordily or nonsensically.

wag, play [v.] Play truant.

waggle Wag.

waggly Unsteady. Loose. Twisting.

waggon, on the Refraining from alcoholic drink.

wakey wakey! Wake up!

walk
1. Take away without permission.
   - *Someone's walked it.* See **walk it** and **walk (it)**.
2. Disappear.
   - *It seems to have walked.*

278

walk away with Win (easily).

walk into Encounter because of lack of forethought.

walk (it) Win easily.

walk it Walk a distance.

walk off with Win (easily).

walk tall Be unashamed, and justifiably proud.

walkabout, (go) (Make) a tour on foot (usu. to meet people). (Of Royal Family, etc.)

wall See **brick wall**.

wall, go, crawl, etc., **up the** Have an angry outburst.

wallah Person. Usu. in hyphenated expressions, e.g. **char-wallah** Person who makes or serves tea.

wallflower Person (usu. female) who attracts no partners at a dance, persons to talk with at a party, etc.

wallop
1. [v.] Hit. Defeat.
2. [n.] Heavy blow.
3. [n.] Drink (usu. beer).
4. **go (down) wallop** Fall heavily.

walloping Very big. Very noticeable.

wally Foolish person.

waltz
1. Move nimbly and gaily. Also **waltz in** Enter.
2. **waltz into** Attack.

wang Penis. Also **wanger**.

wangle
1. [v.] Contrive cunningly or by irregular methods.
2. [n.] Such a contrivance.

wank (off)* Masturbate.

wanker* Disagreeable person.

want Want to get. **want out** Wish to leave (usu. job). **want off** Wish to depart. Etc. with other adverbs.

warm-up [n.] Preparation or entertainment to enliven performers or audience before principal performance begins.

war paint Make-up.

wars, in the In trouble or bother (usu. physical injury).

wash, come out in the Be revealed eventually.

wash, it won't It will not stand up to examination.

wash out [v.] Cancel. Usu. **washed out** Cancelled because of rain.

wash-out [n.] Failure.

washed up Exhausted.

washers Copper coins of the realm.

waster Person who is good for nothing.

watch the dicky bird Look into the lens of the camera. (Expression used when photographing people.)

watcher! Form of greeting. See **wotcher!**

water bewitched Any weak beverage.

watering-hole Public house. Bar.

waterworks Urinary system.

waterworks, turn on the Weep.

wax, in a Angry. [adj.] **waxy** Prone to anger.

way! no Impossible!

way out
  1. Avant-garde; complex; unusual; extreme.
  2. **on the way out** Nearing the end of useful life. About to disappear.

way the cookie crumbles, the See **cookie**.

wear Tolerate. Accept.

weary Willie Tiresome, bored or idle person.

weather See **under the weather**.

weaving, get Begin. Hurry.

wee(-wee) Urination. Also [v.].

weed
1. Tobacco.
2. Dull, feeble person.
3. Marijuana.

weeny Tiny.

weeny-bopper Young **teeny-bopper**.

weepie Highly sentimental film (play, etc.).

weigh in
1. Start. Assist. Intervene.
2. **weigh in with** Introduce.
3. **weigh into** Attack.

weigh up Consider.

weight about, throw one's Exert one's authority or strength. Boast.

weirdo, weirdy Odd, eccentric person. Also same as **beatnik**.

well away, be
1. Be drunk.
2. Be doing very well.

well-heeled Rich.

well in, be Prosper.

well oiled Drunk.

well, what do you know? Excl. of surprise.

wellies Wellington boots.

west, go Be destroyed or killed.

wet
1. (Of person) Feeble. Silly. Dull. Also **talk wet** Talk foolishly.
2. (Of thing, esp. book, film, etc.) Sentimental.
3. **the wet** The rain.
   • *I've been out in the wet.*
4. **wet the baby's head** Celebrate a birth.
4. **a wet** A drink.

wet and sticky, the Difficulties. Embarrassment. Situation from which it is difficult to extricate oneself. Usu. **drop one in the wet and sticky.** Place one in a difficult situation.

wet behind the ears Inexperienced. Young.

wet dream Dream accompanied by sexual emission.

wet one's whistle Have a drink.

wet the tea Make the tea.

whack
1. [n.] Share.
2. [v.] Defeat. Strike.
3. **have a whack at** Attempt.
4. **whacked** Tired out.

whacking Huge. Very.

whacko! Excl. of delight.

whale of a . . . , a A hugely enjoyable . . .

what a hope! Same as **some hope!**

what a life! Excl. of mild disgust.

what do you know! Excl. of surprise. Also form of greeting.

what for, give one Scold (or punish) one.

what gives? Form of greeting. Also, what's happening?

what have you Anything else of that sort.

what it takes, have (got) (Have) the right qualities (for a particular situation).

what the deuce *or* **devil . . . ?** What . . . ? [Emph.]

what the dickens . . . ? What . . . ? [Emph.]

what the doctor ordered What is necessary, suitable, desirable, etc.

what the hell It does not matter.

what's biting *or* **eating you?** What's troubling or annoying you?

what's new? Form of greeting. Also, what's happening?

what's the big idea? See **idea (2)**.

what's what How things ought to be (done) etc.
 • *I'll show them what's what!*

wheel [v.] Bring.

wheeze Joke. Trick. Plan.

where it's at Where something interesting or lively is occurring. [Pop.]

where to get off, tell (show etc.**) one** Tell one an unpalatable fact; (usu. a threat to stop obstructive or troublesome behaviour).
* *I'll tell him where he gets off.* I'll reprimand him.

wherewithal That which is necessary (usu. money).

whip [v.] Steal. See also **crack of the whip**.

whip up Obtain (usu. quickly). Create.
* *I can't whip up much enthusiasm for the idea.*

whirl Attempt. Usu. **give it a whirl**. Try.

whistle, wet one's Have a drink.

whistle for Wish in vain.

whistle-stop [adj.] Stopping briefly at small towns. (App. to electioneering tours, etc.)

whistle up Obtain. Summon.

white-headed boy Favourite.

white man Man of honour.

whitewash
  1. [n.] Vindication, usu. dubious.
  2. [v.] Vindicate. Defeat without allowing opponent to score. Also [n.].

whizz-bang High-velocity shell. Angry letter.

whizz-kid Lively, progressive, successful (young) person.

whodunit Story (film, play, etc.) centring on solution of murder mystery by detection.

whole caboose *or* **caboodle, the** The whole lot.

whole shooting-match, the The whole thing, business, affair.

whoopee!
  1. Excl. of pleasure.
  2. **make whoopee** Enjoy revelry.

whop Thrash. Defeat.

whopper
1. Something huge.
2. Lie.

whopping Huge.

whup Same as **whop**.

wick, get on one's Irritate one.

widdle Same as **piddle**.

wide boy Same as **spiv**.

wide, to the Utterly.

wiggly Not straight.

wild horses wouldn't . . . Nothing would . . .

willies, the Feeling of uneasiness or nervousness.
• *Flying gives me the willies.*

wimp Feeble, foolish, uninteresting person.

win
1. Acquire by theft or finding. Take not quite lawfully or officially.
2. **you can't win (them all)** Expression signifying difficulty of succeeding (always).

winch Move.

wind up
1. [v.] Cause to become angry or lose one's temper.
2. Arrive finally.

wind up, get *or* **have the** Become afraid.

wind up, put the Make afraid or alarmed.

windy [adj.] Afraid. Cowardly.

wingding Wild party.

winge [v.] Grumble (usu. app. to fretful children). [n.] **wingeing.**

wink(ing), like Very quickly.

winning Succeeding. Getting on well. Often in such expressions as
- *Are you winning?*

wino Vagrant with addiction to cheap alcohol.

wipe the floor with Reprimand. Defeat easily.

wire [n.] Telegram. [v.] Telegraph.

wise
1. Informed. Esp. **get** *or* **be wise to** Become or be knowledgeable about (usu. person).
2. **put one wise to** Inform one about. Also **wise (one) up**.

wisecrack
1. [n.] Witty or joking retort.
2. [v.] Make such retort(s).

wise guy Person with unjustifiably high opinion of his own knowledge or of himself.

wish on Give to, provide for, against the wishes of the recipient.

with it [adj.] In the up-to-date fashion in clothes, music, beliefs, tastes, etc.

with it, get *or* **be** Join a fashion; join in, become appreciative of, style. Enjoy oneself.

with knobs on With additions. Used in numerous colloquial rejoinders of sarcastic intention, esp. **same to you, with knobs on** An abusive or facet. reply to an offensive or teasing remark.

with one hand behind one's back, do Do very easily.

with you, I'm not I don't understand you.

witter (on) Talk nonsense at length.

wizard [adj.] Splendid. Very good.

wobbly, throw a Lose one's equanimity. Behave unpredictably.

wodge Same as **wadge**.

wog [n.] Indian or Arab; also Negro. Loosely, any foreigner.
- *The wogs begin at Calais.* [Derog.]

wolf Womaniser.

woman of, make an honest See **honest**.

wonky Unsteady. Defective. Unsound. Unwell.

wood in (the hole), put the Close the door.

wool, lose one's Become angry.

wool on, keep one's Remain calm.

woollies Woollen clothing.

woozy Dizzy with drink.

wop [adj.] & [n.] Italian. [Derog.]

word go, the The beginning.

workaholic Very hard-working person.

work it Bring it about.

work one's finger *or* **trousers to the bone** Work hard.

work over Treat with violence.

work things Arrange matters.

works, give one the Reprimand severely.

world, out of this Extremely good.

worry-guts Habitual worrier.

worse luck So much the worse.

wotcher! Hello!

wow
1. Great success.
2. Impress or entertain greatly.
3. Excl. of surprise or delight.

wrap in cotton wool Mollycoddle. Preserve carefully.

wrap up
1. Stop talking.
2. Conclude (arrangements).

wrapped up Completed. Arranged.

wrinkle Hint, expedient, piece of wisdom, based on experience. Often **give one a few wrinkles** Pass on information or experience to one.

wrong end of the stick, (get) the (Have) a misconception of what has been said, done, etc.

wrong 'un Person of bad character.

wroughty Same as **rorty**.

Y

yakety-yak
1. [n.] Voluble talk.
2. [v.] Talk volubly. Also **yak** [v.].

Yank American.

yap Talk too much. Talk loudly. Complain at length.

Yard, the [Abbr.] (New) Scotland Yard.

yarn
1. Story.
2. [v.] Tell story.
3. **yarn-spinner** Teller of stories.

yawn Something boring.

yeah Yes. Also **oh yeah?** Expression of incredulity.

year dot, the An unspecified date in the distant past.

years on, put [v.] [Lit.] Age. [Met.] Annoy.

yellow
1. Cowardly.
2. **yellow belly** Coward.

yen Intense desire.

yep Yes.

yes-man Sycophant. Subordinate who agrees with everything said by his superior.

Yid Jew. [Derog.]

yippee! Excl. of delight.

yippie Variety of **hippy.**

yob(bo) Lout.

yomp [n.] Forced march. Also [v.].

yonks A long time.

you bet! Most certainly! I agree!

you can say that again I agree.

you don't say! Excl. of surprise (or derision) at a statement.

you have to be joking Expression of refusal or of derisive rejoinder.

you know what thought did Sarcastic rejoinder to one who 'thought' he was not in error.

you, me and the bedpost *or* **lamp-post, between** In confidence.

you must be joking See **joking.**

you said it! That's right!

you're telling me! I know!

you've got a hope! You haven't much chance!

you've said it! See **you said it!**

you've saved my life Emph. expression of thanks.

yours truly I.

yukky Over-rich (in taste). Over-sentimental.

yum-yum! Excl. of pleasurable anticipation.

yummy Attractive. (Of food, girl, etc.)

yuppy Young upwardly mobile (i.e. ambitious) person.

Z

zap [v.] Surprise violently, with a view to hunting or killing.

zing
1. [n.] Liveliness.
2. [v.] Make lively. Usu. **zing up**.

zippy Speedy.

zizz [n.] & [v.] Sleep.

zoom
1. [n.] & [v.] Climb (of aircraft, usu. steep).
2. [v.] Move quickly.

OTHER TITLES AVAILABLE
IN TEACH YOURSELF